Nightmarish Neighborhood #3

The Horrifying History of Buckout Road

by Eric Pleska

WWW.RIGHTONDUDES.COM

WWW.BUCKOUTROAD.COM

CONTENTS

DON'T BE SCARED, BE PREPARED

Be warned: This nonfiction book about Buckout Road may contain disturbing and frightening content. Please proceed with caution.

Named after the once-prominent Buckhout family, Buckout Road in Westchester County has been the site of horrifying history and terrifying urban legends that have been the source of nightmares for generations. Members of the family include Isaac Van Wart Buckhout, who savagely slaughtered his wife and neighbor, resulting in him becoming the last man hanged in White Plains, and Mary Buckhout, whose terrifying ghost is rumored to haunt the road near her burned-down former home and vandalized gravesite.

The unassuming roughly 1.5-mile-long backwoods road was the site of a slave rebellion that led to the largest population of formerly enslaved people in the entire state. It's also where several noteworthy Revolutionary War incidents occurred, including the nearby beheading of a Hessian soldier, which inspired the creation of America's first ghostly phantom, The Headless Horseman.

With its sinister twists and turns, the road leads from the outskirts of the lost village of Kensico, now under the depths of the reservoir that supplies drinking water to the county and New York City, past Woodman's Cove, named after unsolved murder victim Henry Woodman. It then winds its way near a Cold War missile site through the rugged hills of West Harrison, passing through the site of a 19th-century settlement of formerly enslaved people and the sites of eerie incidents and multiple brutal murders.

As the narrow backwoods street flows into White Plains, it runs nearly parallel to Old Orchard Street, where several tragedies occurred near an old stone quarry, and 19th-century farmers reported seeing an unidentified ape-like cryptid creature living near Cranberry Lake. The road passes several cemeteries, all of which vandals and grave robbers have raided, which locals believe may have triggered paranormal activity.

All of this, coupled with a diverse range of eclectic residents, including iconic hermit The Leatherman and America's first horror movie star John Barrymore, an abundance of strange crimes including dozens of arson fires, and a plethora of urban legends involving cannibal albinos, a serial killer, witch executions, a Native American curse, and multiple ghoulish specters, including a vengeful British Revolutionary War captain and "The Lady in White," have helped Buckout Road earn the title of America's scariest street.

1.) SPIRITS OF THE REVOLUTION

Our third *Nightmarish Neighborhood* journey begins relatively close to our previous two expeditions, which explored the lost village of Kensico and uncovered the forgotten history of Old Orchard Street. In fact, they're so close geographically that there is some eventual overlap. Our starting point for this spooky excursion is a popular local delicatessen located on the corner of Kensico Place and Lake Street in a bustling suburban area of White Plains, NY.

Formerly known as E.J.'s Deli, named after former local firefighter Edward "E.J." Lattanzio, who operated the local hot spot in the 1980s, the popular deli has changed names and owners over the years. Its distinctive architecture, built attached to an old house, and its proximity to the populous neighborhoods of "The Valley" and Lake Street apartments near Delfino Park and Ebersole Ice Rink, has made the deli an iconic part of the city for generations.

Across the street from the deli is an I-287 overpass, the site of a terrible accident. In 1994, after an argument with his brother, a young man either slipped or leaped off the muddy embankment and plummeted 50 feet down, crash landing on the busy highway. After a helicopter took him to a nearby hospital, then-deli owner Mike told *The*

Reporter Dispatch he "initially thought nothing of it because people often climb the fence to walk down to the highway."

With the overpass behind you, walking past the deli, up Kensico Place is a right-hand turn onto the beginning of Hall Place, a former Native American footpath.

Hall Avenue has been part of the local landscape for centuries, with a modern history dating back to at least 1721 and a significant rerouting by 1762. The street underwent multiple name changes before becoming Cottage Avenue in the latter half of the 19th century. The street's identity was further shaped when a wealthy man named Aaron Hall bought substantial land in the area, leading to its official Hall Avenue renaming in 1903. Until 2009, before renovations to the Cross-Westchester Expressway, it connected Lake Street with Buckout Road.

During the Revolutionary War, early maps referred to the area of modern-day Hall Avenue as Hatfield Hill. The Hatfields in America descend from Thomas Hatfield of Mamaroneck, NY and his brother Matthias, who settled in Massachusetts after emigrating from Nottinghamshire in England.

Family members include the Hatfields of the infamous Hatfield and McCoy feud in the West Virginia—Kentucky area, Eduard Hatfield, whose farmland once occupied the area east of Silver Lake to North Broadway, including all of modern-day Delfino Park, and Abraham Hatfield, who operated a Loyalist tavern in downtown White Plains.

During the 1770s, Abraham's son, 20-something-year-old American Patriot Gilbert Hatfield, lived in a farmhouse on what is now Hall Ave.

He fought in the local militia against the British, and during the Revolutionary War in 1776, Continental Army General William Heath made his headquarters there.

On the evening of October 27, 1776, the woods of Hatfield Hill, encompassing modern-day Hall Ave and Buckout Road, which Hall Avenue eventually turns into, became littered with tents, blankets, and campfires. It's where the left flank of George Washington's Continental Army camped before the historic Battle of White Plains against the British Army.

The soldiers were provided a weekly ration of food, which typically included 1 pound of bread, ½ pound of beef, ½ pound of pork, 1 pint of milk, ½ a pint of vinegar, 6 ounces of butter, ½ cup of peas or beans, and a quart of malt beer. For some of these men, it was to be their last meal. With battle looming in the hours ahead, some of these men went to sleep, knowing they might not survive to have another night's rest. For these brave men, their last moment of peace was in the woods of Hatfield Hill.

The following day, the opening shots fired a short distance away on what is now called Battle Hill. Washington's army, dressed in blue, was armed with muskets, bayonets, and cannons. The Continental Army had tangled with General Howe's British Army before, but it was the first time they had to fight the combination of the redcoats and their hired highly skilled German mercenary warriors, the Hessians.

Washington deployed his army along a three-mile-wide line. He commanded the center flank, Major General Israel Putnam commanded the right side, and General William Heath led the left. The gruesome clash lasted for about thirty minutes.

While considered a British victory, Howe failed to capture Washington and end the Revolution. The battle marked the arrival of the Hessians as a significant fighting force. It helped establish the careers of several people, including a Patriot spy named Benjamin Tallmadge and a young artillery captain named Alexander Hamilton. Some historians estimate that 450 lives were lost that day. The abundance of injuries led to the creation of numerous makeshift hospitals, including one at the Quaker meeting house adjacent to Buckout Road.

Additional skirmishes and fights continued over the days ahead, including an incident where four Hessian privates attacked Gilbert Hatfield in what was called "in a lonely place" thought to be on Buckout Road. The report states:

Two of them grabbed Hatfield, demanding his money. They discovered their mistake when the American youth tripped both of them, knocked the other two down, and proceeded to beat all four of them. He reported his assailants to the Hessian commander, who offered to make an example of these soldiers but relented when found that they had already had plenty of punishment.

That Halloween night, October 31, 1776, General Washington used the camouflage of a roaring thunderstorm to stealthily relocate his central detachment of the Continental Army to nearby Wright's Mills at the modern-day site of Kensico Dam Plaza.

Meanwhile, other parts of the army relocated to nearby high ground, including Miller Hill and Mt. Misery, where they set up defenses. General Heath and a detachment of soldiers under his command remained on Hatfield Hill, setting up defenses to guard nearby supply depots and track enemy movements. Gilbert Hatfield's farmhouse sat strategically high on Hatfield Hill about 400 feet away from a large granite ledge, referred to early maps as "Muckle Stone Rock" near the "Indian Line of Marked Trees."

Local legend is that on that stormy Halloween night of 1776, a British officer named Captain Tilton attempted to kill General Heath. Tilton chased Heath through the nearby woods, trying to fatally stab him with a 62-inch long musket armed with a razor-sharp bayonet on its muzzle. As they sprinted through the woods, they neared the northern border of the Hatfield property, where Heath found refuge while his comrades tried to apprehend Captain Tilton.

According to research published by a reverend from the White Plains Presbyterian Church, Captain Tilton, while being pursued by American soldiers and unaware of the abrupt ending of the rocky platform, plunged off the cliff into the ravine below and was killed. Because of the Captain's tragic fate, Muckle Stone Rock was sometimes called "Tilton's Rock."

From this Revolutionary War era tale, an early eerie urban legend arose that on Halloween night, if you're near Muckle Stone Rock, you may catch a ghostly glimpse of the phantom British officer pussyfooting through the woods, searching for his target, General Heath. Some local ghost hunters believe solid, thick white orbs in photographs near his fatal tumble may be the Captain's spirit trying to make contact. Others have claimed to hear mysterious groans thought to be Captain Tilton's ghost begging for help out of Mucklestone Rock.

A woman who grew up in the area, Diane, recalls that in the 1950s, her grandfather purchased the Hatfield house on Hall Avenue. Her family tradition is that during the Revolutionary War, the house was not just the headquarters for General Heath but that it also hosted a famous guest, General George Washington.

 Various artifacts from the war, including musket balls, buttons, and cannonballs, have been found on and around the property over the years. The Hatfield house on 1020 Hall Avenue was one of the oldest houses in Westchester County until 2012 when a real estate company demolished it.

2.) THE UNSOLVED MURDER OF ISABELLE

A century after Revolutionary War soldiers occupied the street, Hall Avenue, then known as Cottage Ave, became the site of a mysterious unsolved murder.

On Wednesday, January 22, 1902, Isabelle Allen, a wife and mother of five, strangely did not come home after a routine work day on Mamaroneck Ave in downtown White Plains. Later that evening, her worried husband James and 20-year-old daughter Isabella visited the house of Isabelle's employer. He confirmed she left work hours ago, at 6:15 pm, as usual.

That night and into the early hours of the next morning, the worried Allen family, their Cottage Avenue neighbors, and the police scoured the area looking for the missing woman. After a sixteen-hour-long search, a delivery boy named Eugene Harders made a gruesome discovery.

After dropping off groceries to August Sonberg, a few hundred feet from the Allens' house on the same narrow street, he started to back his horse to turn his wagon around. The hind wheels struck something, and the boy exited the wagon to see what it was. Behind a clump of bushes next to a stone wall about five feet from the road was a dead body.

Eugene rushed to alert the Sonbergs, who identified the body as Isabelle Allen and notified the police. The victim had a sizeable gash on her cheek and substantial bruising throughout her body. Her face was almost unrecognizable after sustaining a terrible beating.

The police found her empty pocketbook on the other side of a fence near her body. Thirty feet from her body, a boy named Ed Still found her eyeglasses. Investigators found a small flannel bag she often wore a short distance away, torn in several pieces. Inside the bag was a bible.

The police arrested Isabelle's husband, James, a stone mason and former sea captain, for the murder of his wife. They believed the motive might have been financial, as Isabelle was the descendant of a prominent Spanish family. However, after a hearing where James provided an alibi that his daughter and four sons corroborated, they released him.

A few hours after the police released James, they arrested another local man for Mrs. Allen's murder named Cloyd Barker. He was a Black resident of the nearby Stony Hill section of Buckout Road. The police said he was one of the first people on the scene when Mrs. Allen's body was discovered, and he seemed very anxious and asked the police several times if he could be of any assistance.

The police were familiar with Cloyd, who had been jailed numerous times for various crimes, including a nine-year prison sentence at Sing Sing after a brutal incident that took place just up the street on Buckout Road. In 1879, Cloyd got into a heated fight with his father, Civil War veteran David Barker. Cloyd knocked out his father and repeatedly smashed a stone over his head, leaving his father missing an eye and clinging to his life.

With Cloyd's criminal history, especially his usage of a stone to beat his father's face, the police believed Cloyd was Mrs. Allen's murderer. However, after a lack of evidence connecting him to the crime, they released him.

The police stayed busy and soon arrested another man for Mrs. Allen's murder. The suspect was an Italian named Leopoldo, who, after a lack of evidence, they also released.

The investigation continued. Near the crime scene, the police discovered a pair of men's shoes and a piece of an envelope containing the address of another Italian man, stone mason Salvatore Falzarono, who lived around the corner on Kensico Ave. The police arrested him.

Salvatore gave an alibi but contradicted himself numerous times. When investigators produced the shoes found at the crime scene, which appeared to be of similar size to the one Salvatore wore, he refused to put them on. Suspicions of Salvatore grew even more after Mrs. Allen's daughter Isabella, and two other young girls from the neighborhood, Alice Stanfield and Julia Nelson, told police that they were certain Salvatore had previously followed and annoyed them.

Eventually, due to a lack of evidence connecting him to the crime, the court discharged Salvatore for Isabelle's murder. During questioning, however, Salvatore implicated himself in another matter.

A year earlier, the police issued an arrest warrant for an Italian man named Tony Sandillo, wanted for murdering a man named Michael Salerno in Tuckahoe. Tony somehow evaded capture until Salvatore bragged that he not only knew where Tony was hiding, but he helped him flee the country to Naples, Italy, to avoid the charges. As a result, the police held Salvatore to await an investigation by the District Attorney.

A few days later, the police arrested another man for Isabelle Allen's murder. This time, they charged a 24-year-old Black man named Frank Boyd from the Stony Hill section of Buckout Road. The police picked him up at his mother's house near St. Luke's A.M.E. Church on Westchester Avenue.

The arrest came after witnesses told police that Boyd and another Black man from Stony Hill named Peter Beverly boarded a trolley near the crime scene on the night of Isabelle's murder.

The police were acquainted with Mr. Beverly after an incident a few years prior. In June 1896, local gossip emerged that a Stony Hill man named Charles Sickles shot and killed Peter Beverly. When police investigated, they found Sickles at his home with a sore arm, and to their surprise, they also found Beverly at home, unhurt. It's unclear how those rumors started, but from their prior interactions, the police believed Mr. Beverly to be an honest man.

When questioned, he told police he met Boyd on Lake Street on the night in question, between Cottage Ave and Maglio's Hotel. He said Boyd had been drinking and told him that he had committed a crime, that he "knocked out a woman, struck her harder than intended."

While Frank Boyd sat in jail awaiting trial, the public believed the police had successfully arrested Isabelle's murderer. Multiple witnesses testified against Boyd at trial, including Peter Beverly and Frank's brother William, who corroborated Peter's testimony. The prisoner did not testify to his defense.

On April 29, 1902, despite the evidence against Frank Boyd, the jury acquitted him of all charges, and the police released him.

It remains unknown whether the police arrested the right man or not. That July, Frank Boyd and a man from Yonkers named George, who went by multiple aliases, burglarized the home of 78-year-old Margaret Kelly. She lived on Westchester Ave near Ophir Farm. During the home invasion, Frank knocked Mrs. Kelly unconscious after striking her repeatedly in the head with a stone wrapped in a handkerchief.

Residents from the neighborhood formed a posse and tried to apprehend the two crooks, but they escaped into the woods. The police captured them a few days later. At trial, Judge Platt sentenced Frank Boyd to a $1,000 fine (about $35,000 today) and a five-year prison sentence at Sing Sing.

The murder of Isabelle Allen on Cottage Ave remains unsolved.

3.)MURDER OR SELF DEFENSE

Shortly after Cottage Avenue became renamed Hall Avenue, new suburban homes sprouted up and began to decorate the tranquil scenery along the quiet street where, decades earlier, someone got away with murder.

However, three of these Hall Avenue houses were at one time occupied by an individual arrested by the police for murder. In each case, the accused killer maintained they acted in self-defense.

I.)

In late July 1968, a Port Chester man named Horace Lewis allegedly assaulted a Rye woman named Renee Campbell and her two-month-old daughter, who needed five stitches after sustaining a head injury. Renee reportedly responded by slashing Horace, causing him to receive multiple stitches for the knife wounds. It's unclear what their relationship was or what provoked the incident.

Two weeks later, Renee's fiancée, 22-year-old Hall Avenue resident Vernon Eugene Calloway, went to Horace's apartment. It's unknown what exactly transpired. However, the result was that the police arrested Vernon for stabbing Horace eighteen times, killing him. Vernon maintained that he acted in self-defense after Horace struck him in the face with a blunt object.

II.)

In April 1970, local newspapers reported that a 27-year-old Corrections Department officer who lived on Hall Avenue got into an altercation with a former police officer from Trinidad named Beresford Riley following a minor car accident in Port Chester. The corrections officer, Kenneth Chamberlain, claimed Riley and two passengers in his car threatened him. An altercation ensued, resulting in Chamberlain firing a single round from a .38 caliber service revolver. The bullet passed through Riley's heart, and shortly after, he died.

The police arrested Chamberlain and charged him with manslaughter. After a long investigation and a lengthy trial, Chamberlain's trial resulted in a hung jury and acquittal.

In 2011, a tragic event that made national news happened on South Lexington Ave in White Plains; 68-year-old Kenneth Chamberlain's medical alert was accidentally triggered, resulting in an early morning wellness check by several officers of the White Plains police department.

Conflicting reports emerged about what happened next, though it appears the police who responded to the medical alert tried to gain entry into Chamberlain's apartment to verify his condition. At the same time, Mr. Chamberlain, in a state of desperation, repeatedly told officers he did not need help and asked the police to leave him alone.

It was reported that a 90-minute verbal standoff ensued, intensifying the situation. This prolonged interaction, which may have included a police officer using racist remarks, culminated in the police attempting to forcibly enter Mr. Chamberlain's apartment. According to reports, as the police began to open Mr. Chamberlain's apartment door forcibly, he responded by defensively wielding a knife through the door's opening.

After busting down the door and gaining entry into the apartment, the police used a taser on Mr. Chamberlain, who suffered from a heart condition. There are conflicting reports about what happened next, but an officer fired two gunshots at Mr. Chamberlain, killing him.

 A Westchester grand jury later voted not to charge any of the officers in the incident, including the purported shooter. The victim's son filed a civil suit for $21M against the city of White Plains and its police department, which went to trial, but the jury found neither accused party liable for damages.

 In January 2015, one of the officers involved in the incident, Steven Hart, died in a fiery car crash in Poughkeepsie. Police reported his car "left the roadway at a high rate of speed, went into the woods, struck a tree, and caught fire." Hart was 39.

 In 2019, the events leading to Kenneth Chamberlain's death were portrayed in the movie *The Killing of Kenneth Chamberlain*, which is available on multiple platforms, including Prime Video. The film stars Frankie Faison as the titular Kenneth Chamberlain.

 In August 2023, the city of White Plains reportedly reached a settlement with Kenneth Chamberlain's family for $5M.

III.)

In December 1985, White Plains police arrested a 28-year-old woman who lived on Hall Avenue and charged her with the brutal murder of her 45-year-old brother, known locally by his nickname "Charlie Brown."

 What prompted the dispute between the siblings at the victim's downtown White Plains apartment on South Lexington Ave that December evening is unclear. At some point during the night, the siblings attended a party on the seventh floor of the apartment complex. A commotion ensued later that night, leading to a police presence.

 When the police arrived, they found "Charlie Brown" stabbed to death. They arrested his sister for the murder.

 A month later, a Westchester County Court judge found the 28-year-old woman guilty of manslaughter with a sentence of up to 25 years in prison. She contended the stabbing occurred in self-defense and alternately that her brother stumbled into the knife.

4.)BALDWIN FARM

Located near the site of Isabelle Allen's century-old unsolved murder, a modern sign on Hall Avenue marks the entrance to Baldwin Farm. Behind the large marker once stood the last working farm in White Plains.

From its humble origins as a two-acre home on 67 Hall Avenue, established in 1823 by John Foster and his wife, Mary Marsh Foster, this property underwent a remarkable metamorphosis. Fueled by their unyielding determination and dedication, the modest farmhouse John constructed with wood from his land blossomed into a thriving 22-acre farm, serving as a haven for their large family of 12 children, numerous animals, and many crops. This transformation is a testament to the willful spirit and adaptability of the area's settlers after the American Revolution.

One significant event in the farm's history was a 90-foot pine tree falling on the property during a storm. This event, which could have been a disaster, became a stroke of luck. Miraculously, the tree narrowly missed the Foster house, sparing the family from potential harm. This incident led the family to affectionately refer to the farm as Pine Tree Farm, a name that would stick for generations.

John Foster's oldest daughter, Deborah, was the first to leave the farm after her marriage to a Quaker man named Frederick Stephens (also sometimes spelled Federick Stevens). The couple, however, lived close by, just up the street on Buckout Road. John's daughter Elizabeth Ann also remained close after her marriage to local carpenter and military veteran John Quincy Adams Buckhout, who also lived up the road on the street named after his family.

After John's wife, Elizabeth, died in 1834, the Pine Tree Farm property extended up the curvy and hilly road to include a small cemetery. The family explained that it was the only road in White Plains laid out by a cow. The cows took the easiest path into the woods, often retracing the steps of an ancient Siwanoy trail. The cow path eventually became Cottage Avenue (later Hall Avenue) and The Road to The Hills, later renamed Buckhout Road and then Buckout Road.

John Foster died at Pine Tree Farm in 1841. His family paid local undertaker Robert Murdock $13 for headstones and gravedigger John Farrington $1 for digging John's grave next to his wife. John left part of his land to his son, William, and the rest to his oldest son, James.

The Foster children embraced the family farming tradition, with James successfully operating the farm with his family until his passing in 1862. Shortly after, his daughter Sarah and her husband, Horace Baldwin, purchased the Hall Ave property from James' widow, Mary Foster, for $3,000 and renamed it Baldwin Farm.

Despite the initial struggles of transitioning from a New York City stagecoach driver to a White Plains farmer, Horace became connected to the property. He even added a meticulously constructed carriage house to the property in 1884. The rich family farming tradition endured, with Sarah and Horace's only child, Charles Baldwin, eventually assuming control after the passing of his mom in 1902 and father in 1903

Each generation, deeply rooted in the land, nurtured the farm with love and dedication. At its peak, Baldwin Farm was not just a family home but a bustling hub of economic activity. It was home to a diverse array of livestock, including cows, horses, a bull, 100 chickens, and a tame raccoon named Sandy. The farm also boasted a sprawling apple orchard and a cider mill. The family sold goods and produce from their farm to local shops, contributing to the local economy and the community's well-being.

In 1907, Charles Baldwin developed a water supply, transporting water from a spring via gravity into the house's kitchen and bathroom. He expanded the original house a year later, adding three new rooms.

The Baldwin house stood proudly next to other structures, including several barns, a woodshed, a grainary, a smokehouse, and a large barn across the street. This impressive array of infrastructure is a testament to the farm's prosperity and the Baldwin family's dedication.

Wood-burning stoves heated the house, including one in the kitchen, where Charles' wife, Ellen Maginnis Foster, who emigrated from Newcastle, County Down, Ireland, did the family's cooking. While not farming, Charles became one of the first members of the Union Hook and Ladder Company.

The Fosters' first child, Sarah, died unexpectedly in 1940 at age 47. The White Plains High School graduate was a member of the White Plains Presbyterian Church, worked as a stenographer, and later worked at a law office. She was survived by her parents, a sister named Clarissa, and younger brother David.

Growing up in White Plains, David Baldwin attended Eastview School during the early 1900s and delivered milk on Mitchell Place for five cents a gallon before school. He played baseball on The Hilltops, named for the hill overlooking Lake Street. As an adult, he smoked cigars and, while not a drinker, would sometimes stop in a bar solely to hear the news that wasn't in the newspapers. Throughout his life, most of all, David enjoyed caring for his animals and helping his father.

In 1953, the police arrested David after he fired a shotgun at several youths who decided to play baseball on Baldwin Farm. After his father, Charles, posted bail, the judge eventually dropped the charges and ordered David to remove all guns from the property.

Ellen Baldwin died in 1955, and her husband, farmer Charles Baldwin, passed away a few years later, on August 24, 1959, at his home, where he had been born 94 years prior. After Charles' death, David and his sister Clarissa took over the operations of the last surviving farm in White Plains.

Things remained relatively peaceful, except a few times when neighbors on nearby Grant Avenue called the police because of loose cows from the farm roaming in front of their homes. In 1966, the police rushed to Baldwin Farm, where they took 70-year-old David to St. Agnes Hospital for medical treatment after the farm's bull had gored him. After fracturing his ribs and receiving 19 stitches on his face, David sold the bull.

A year later, firefighters rushed to the farm after a small fire was caused by the chimney getting too hot from bread baking in the wood-burning stove.

In 1967, the White Plains Recreation Advisory Committee discussed possibly leasing Baldwin Farm and turning it into a children's animal farm, though the plans never advanced.

After Clarissa died in 1969, David, who never married or had children, remained at Baldwin Farm alone. The police visited once that summer after a neighbor complained that he had hung an American flag upside down to protest the current events of 1969.

In 1971, an arson fire destroyed two of the Baldwin Farm barns, injuring animals and killing a cow. The police did not make any arrests.

A neighbor named Rick recalled:

"I lived right next to Baldwin's Farm, was at the fire when I was 4, saw the charred cow, and others that survived milled about the farms for years to come with terrible burns on their sides, like giant walking t-bone steaks."

A couple of years later, in 1973, the city of White Plains purchased the property for $300,000, intending to turn it into a public park. The city agreed to pay David $200 monthly in caretaker's fees to tend the farm for the rest of his life.

Farmer David Baldwin remained living at the now-city-owned farm until December 5, 1979. He had just finished preparing hay to feed the cows on his farm and visited with friends Henry and William Borman, who stopped by with a candy box as an early Christmas present. About half an hour later, 88-year-old David died while carrying coal from his truck to a wood-burning stove inside the two-story wood-frame home.

Like his father, Charles Baldwin, grandfather, Horace Baldwin, great-grandfather, James Foster, and great-great-grandfather, John Foster, David Baldwin, the last of a family of farmers, lived and died on the farm he loved.

While walking home from Eastview Junior High School, Wayne Slaughter found David Baldwin's body.

"He was lying on his front step with his dog beside him. I can see it like it was yesterday."

Neighbor Rick recalled:

"He was laid out in a cross shape in front of the porch, eyes open, gone. I used to feel something looking at me from the window on the house's third floor, facing west, which I could see from my bathroom window, a dark hole of terror."

Other locals recall that David had no television and hardly answered his telephone. One neighbor even said that by the late 1970s, the house lacked furniture and "was covered with weird geometric drawings."

Another neighbor, Marianne, recounted:

"He was not crazy, but he did curse children and teens because they harmed his animals and maliciously pranked him. I happened to have a friendship with him and his sister. I would bring them chocolate chip cookies I had baked, and we'd occasionally talk."

David was buried next to his sister Clarissa at the White Plains Rural Cemetery on North Broadway, next to the Presbyterian Church, where they were both members. As per his will, all of the farm's animals and his personal possessions were auctioned off, and the proceeds went to the church. One of his most prized possessions was a pre-Civil War handwritten letter by Secretary Of State Jefferson Davis excusing his grandfather Horace from the service.

Before he died, David expressed his desire to see Baldwin Farm turned into a museum that offers lectures and tours for children. He hoped the city could use the farm's acreage for a tree farm and nature conservatory.

Despite the city of White Plains owning the farm, by 1981, it had become overgrown with vines and weeds. The porch sagged, and animal droppings littered the farmhouse's interior.

That June, the White Plains Youth Employment Service hired twenty teens from White Plains to bring the farm back to life. They painted and cleaned the house, mowed the grass, and cut the weeds and vines from the old stone wall surrounding the property. The youths reinforced the porch, cleaned the farmhouse, and hung an American flag on the newly repaired flagpole right side up.

In late August 1982, vandals set the Baldwin Farmhouse on fire. The unprovoked arson blaze left several cows with burn marks and burned the century-and-a-half-old farmhouse that housed Fosters and Baldwins for generations to the ground.

After an investigation, the police arrested the culprits who destroyed Baldwin Farm, a 38-year-old White Plains Water Department maintenance man named John J Walker Jr and his 14-year-old son. The police said they lit the fire because they "got a kick of it."

After probing further, the police arrested a 19-year-old from White Plains for a role in the Baldwin Farm fire and two youths from Greenburgh who partook in other local arson fires with the maintenance man and his son.

Investigators believe the group of youths piled into the ringleader's 1974 brown Cadillac to commit various acts of arson, including firebombing several automobiles and a vacant apartment, torching Mohawk Day Camp in Greenburgh, and throwing Molotov cocktails through a window of a Greenburgh home, forcing its inhabitants to race to safety, narrowly avoiding death.

Detectives said that although not every group member participated in every fire, all the cases were intertwined; some were done by two participants, some by four.

The two Greenburgh youths pleaded guilty to arson charges. In September 1983, the judge indicated he would sentence them to 3-12 and 5-15 years, respectively. After pleading guilty to multiple arson charges and stealing a motorcycle, the judge said the ringleader, John, would be sentenced to serve 4-12 years.

While awaiting his November 22, 1983 sentencing, a new family moved into John's house on Cloverdale Avenue in White Plains. While cleaning the basement, the new homeowner discovered a strange metal object, leading him to call the police, who determined it was a World War II aerial bomb.

The Westchester County Police Bomb Squad removed the 25-pound bowling pin-shaped weapon. They transported it to a police explosives bunker in Hawthorne, NY, where they stored it until being taken to an artillery range at West Point Military Academy to be detonated.

By 1984, a community garden program began at Baldwin Farm, with 55 plots of 20x20 foot farmland available to citizen gardeners. That August, White Plains Park Commissioner Joseph Davidson told *The Report Dispatch* that the project became so popular that there was a waiting list of people hoping to have one of the plots to grow their own plants and vegetables.

Commissioner Davidson explained that

"White Plains saw Baldwin Farm's potential and devised a plan to create a green spot in an ever-graying city. The state Department of Recreation and Parks agreed to turn over to the city a $100,000 federal grant that would help turn the farm into a natural museum for city residents to learn about farming as it once was in White Plains. But,

then disaster struck when arsonists destroyed the main farmhouse, which was to have been the center of the park plan."

On Monday night, September 7, 1987, firefighters rushed to Baldwin Farm to extinguish a fire. When they arrived at 10:21 p.m., they discovered a large barn engulfed in flames. Five minutes later, it collapsed. Investigators deemed it suspicious because the wood structure, which stood isolated on the sprawling farm, had no electricity, and there were no signs that the fire was accidental.

In August 1988, *The Reporter Dispatch* printed the obituary of John Walker's son. It said he died of pneumonia at his home in Stamford, CT. He was 20 years old, working as a tow truck driver and living with his mother and her new husband. The obituary said he "moved to Stamford to live with his mother when his father died in 1983."

In September 1992, the White Plains police arrested two men for third-degree insurance fraud. The police unraveled the scheme, in which one of the men drove a 1990 Mustang along Hall Avenue before stashing it on Baldwin Farm. Meanwhile, the other participant reported the car stolen. Police then watched the men trespass onto Baldwin Farm and begin stripping the car of its parts, with the intent of selling off the parts, burning the car, and collecting the insurance money.

In 2016, the Baldwin Farm area in White Plains was so overgrown with weeds and poison ivy that the city 'hired' a herd of 29 goats to help. These goats, who became temporary residents of the farm, were often seen near the road's edge, drawing the attention of passer-byers. Their story took an unexpected turn when they managed to escape from their enclosure, leading to several television appearances on Local News 12. This daring escape added a touch of intrigue to their already quirky story.

Today, the goats, their flimsy enclosure, and maybe any memory of the local history are gone. The community garden project remains active, eventually adding a honey bee hive and a new "Community Garden" sign in 2020. The Parks & Rec Department can provide instructions on how to obtain a gardening permit by calling 914-422-1336.

Whether actual or imagined, some people have claimed to see the apparition of a man dressed in overalls between Baldwin Farm and the nearby cemetery. Reports of chills and nausea when spotting the phantom farmer are allegedly standard. All five male "Farmer Fosters" (John and James) and "Farmer Baldwins" (Horace, Charles, and David) died on the farm's property.

According to local lore, Mary Foster allegedly hanged herself in a Quaker church that used to be near the farm's property. Some believe her spirit still roams the property where she and her family once lived in peace and near her gravesite, just up the road.

5.)THE BURIAL GROUND

Exiting Baldwin Farm's grounds and turning right to proceed up Hall Avenue leads to additional sites of horror and intrigue. The first intersection is Lakeview Drive, just a few yards away.

Lakeview Drive is the top part of the tiny Westminster Ridge neighborhood. As discussed in *Nightmarish Neighborhood #2 Old Orchard Street*, the former low-cost-housing neighborhood features a couple of blocks of homes near its focal point, Todd's Pond. The waterhole, which used to be a polluted dumping ground, has been the site of multiple tragedies, including three documented drowning deaths.

In January 1964, the police arrested a man in Westminster Ridge after he murdered his wife, Linda Olmestead Paynter, outside of her home on Westminster Ave. They found him sobbing on a snow bank, holding a bent, bloody knife over his wife's dead body. He told the police he tried to kill himself, but the blade bent. The Westminster Ridge neighborhood connects with Orchard Street, which leads to Old Orchard Street, a road packed with history and haunts that, for a stretch, runs roughly parallel to Buckout Road.

Proceeding along Hall Avenue, the road switches names near the next intersection, Woodale Avenue, to Buckout Road. Near this point is Gilbert Hatfield's former home, which served as a Revolutionary War headquarters for General Heath of the Continental Army. Near this is the alleged site where redcoat Captain Tilton plunged to his death off Muckle Stone Rock.

Developers destroyed the Hatfield house around 2012. The historical house's property became divided into multiple lots where developers built new homes. A few doors down from there is the site of an infamous urban legend referred to locally as Mary's Lantern.

A statue of Mary on someone's lawn once held a lantern. According to the legend, if Mary's lantern is lit, then it's safe to proceed along Buckout Road. But if the lantern is not lit, you're being warned of potential danger ahead. The legend suggests that the lantern is powered by either the wandering spirit of Captain Tilton or by the ghost of Mary Buckhout, who used to reside up the road. According to rumor, someone eventually shot Mary's arm off with a BB gun, destroying the lantern.

Proceeding up the road, on the left side, is a small cemetery that was once part of the Baldwin Farm property. The road by the cemetery used to be narrow and steep. In the early 2000s, it was leveled and widened.

John Foster's sons initially built the cemetery's stone walls around 1841. Immediately visible beyond the cemetery wall is the large gravestone belonging to John F. Buckhout and his wife, Charlotte Cowan Buckhout.

Born in 1847, John grew up on Buckout Road (formerly known as Buckhout Road), named after his family. His father, military captain John Quincy Adams Buckhout, worked as a carpenter and operated a farm up the road. John F. Buckhout's middle name, Foster, is an homage to his Foster family relatives, who used to operate Pine Tree Farm, which became Baldwin Farm. John F. Buckhout's mother was Elizabeth Ann Foster Buckhout, the daughter of Pine Tree Farm founder John Foster.

John had three siblings: an older sister, Mary; a brother, Isaac, who died when he was 19 (not the "Mad Murderer of Sleepy Hollow," discussed at length in *Nightmarish Neighborhood #4*); and a baby sister named Nancy, who passed away before her second birthday. He also had half-siblings through his father's first marriage, which saw the birth of sixteen children.

In 1871, John married Charlotte Cowan, a half-Irish and half-Canadian girl from White Plains. The couple had four children: Albert, Charles, Lilly, and youngest Emma, who went by the nickname Gracie. John worked as a carpenter and later served as a Harrison Justice of the Peace. He eventually relocated his family to Springdale, Connecticut, where he became involved in real estate.

When John died in 1915, his family buried him in the small cemetery where Hall Avenue meets Buckout Road, a place with which he had a great connection. Not just because he used to live on the road but also because several dozen of his family members were laid to rest there, a total of at least 53 burials.

Despite the single gravestone belonging to John F. Buckhout and his wife Charlotte, who died in 1927, the cemetery has at least 54 burials, dating back to John Foster in 1841.

Known as "The Foster / Buckhout Family Burial Ground," members of both families, including John Q.A. Buckhout, Elizabeth Foster Buckhout, and others, were laid to rest here, along with members of other families, who, like the Buckhouts, are intertwined with the Foster family through marriages. These include members from the Carpenter, Cox, Meeks, Platt, Stephens, and Wildey families, including former Harrison Justice of the Peace Caleb Wildey, who, in 1948, became the cemetery's most recent burial. The Wildey family originated in Tarrytown and is the namesake of "Wildey Swamp," popularized in Washington Irving's "Legend of Sleepy Hollow."

Amongst the cemetery's burials are Epenetus Platt and multiple members of the Meeks family, including Isaac, Mary G., Joseph, William, Moses, Solomon, and Mary L. However, by 1943, when local historian Richard Lander surveyed the cemetery, those gravestones were all missing or destroyed.

Moses and Solomon Meeks were twin brothers; Solomon was the husband of Mary L. Meeks, formerly Mary L. Buckhout, the sister of John F. Buckhout. Mary is the subject of several eerie urban legends associated with Buckout Road.

In one gruesome and potentially baseless version, Mary murdered her three children and hid their hearts under the floorboards of her house, which she sat over in her rocking chair until succumbing to a fatal mental illness. In another chilling version, Mary's husband, Solomon Meeks, murdered their three children and hid their bodies. Mary searched unsuccessfully for her children's remains before dying from a mental illness in 1896.

In another creepy version, after being buried in the Foster/Buckhout Cemetery next to her former husband, Mary's ghost allegedly rose from the dead as she refused to stop searching for her children. Some locals have claimed to see her ghost, described as wearing all white, on various Buckout Road properties, perhaps searching for her children.

Some even believe the popular "Bloody Mary" urban legend originated with Mary Buckhout. While it remains unclear if her ghostly image will appear in your bathroom mirror after repeating a phrase numerous times while splashing water, flickering lights, and flushing a toilet, there have been multiple alleged ghost sightings near the graveyard. Many older residents have recalled seeing her gravesite disrupted and dug up, which people feel perhaps triggered paranormal activity.

Additionally, the spirit of Mary Foster, locally known as "The Lady in White," who local lore says hanged herself in a nearby Quaker church, also purportedly roams the area between her former home, Pine Tree Farm, and the burial ground.

Photographs of the cemetery from 1957, on file with the Westchester County Historical Society, didn't capture any orbs or plasmas but do show the bases of eight gravesites with missing headstones amongst the remaining rows of thin, white headstones and a handful of smaller ones, low to the ground.

In March 1963, *The Reporter Dispatch* reported that vandals damaged several plots in the cemetery.

Photographs of the cemetery from 1974 on file with the Westchester County Historical Society show that that city added a lamppost in the middle of the burial ground, perhaps intending to defer future vandalism. Unfortunately, that didn't seem to pan out as planned, as by 1974, multiple other headstones had been stolen or vandalized.

A horrified resident living near the cemetery phoned the police in December 1977 after noticing a ghoulish raid in the burial ground. When the police investigated, they found numerous disturbances, including a five-foot hole in one section of the neglected graveyard near the overturned grave of John and Charlotte Buckhout.

Police captain Patrick Gleason told *The Reporter Dispatch* "There's a distinct possibility that the remains of (John F.) Buckhout and his wife may have been removed. In addition, several headstones are missing from the graveyard."

The police theorize that the grave robbers who plundered the cemetery might have been searching for jewelry on bodies, or, as an officer told the newspaper, "they might have been cultists stealing skulls or remains, a practice reported in the recent arrest of four people in Queens, who were said to be using remains in witchcraft ceremonies." Detectives said vandals and fortune hunters have plagued the cemetery, searching for valuable artifacts such as gold fillings from teeth. They said that despite the cemetery being overgrown with knee-high grass and thorny shrubbery, some even visit the graveyard with metal detection devices.

The police did not dig further down into the gravesite to find out for sure if vandals stole the Buckhout's casket or corpses. A few days later, the Department of Public Works filled the hole. They noted that vandals spray painted names on the cemetery walls in spray paint and that soda cans and old tires littered the ground. The police made no arrests.

Farmer David Baldwin declined to comment to *The Reporter Dispatch* on the matter except to say that vandals have raided the cemetery in the past. Afterward, rumors spread that some missing headstones appeared scattered on Baldwin Farm. Another rumor is that two corpses appeared on the farm posed as scarecrows.

Shortly after, additional rumors emerged that local historians, the Cerak brothers, who lived on Buckout Road, removed the remaining headstones from the cemetery with good intentions to avoid them from being stolen. It's rumored those headstones are still in the possession of the Westchester Historical Society, perhaps sitting in an Elmsford office closet. They have declined to comment despite numerous emails and phone messages.

In June 2001, the local newspaper *The Journal News* published an article, "Cemetery Gets City's Attention," speaking with White Plains Mayor Joseph Delfino and North Castle Historical Society trustee Barbara Massi confirmed the city of White Plains would be erecting a monument containing the names of everyone buried in the Foster / Buckhout burial ground.

"The city of White Plains is now pledging to pay for a new marker or monument that will name the 43 people who are known to have been buried in the Buckhout Cemetery. Since the 1820s, the cemetery has held the remains of several well-known families from White Plains – Foster, Baldwin, and Buckhout. The single monument will serve as a modern-day replacement for the 40 or so headstones that were lost to vandals and thieves through the years, though a few surviving headstones are said to be kept in private hands for safekeeping."

A local resident named Tom recalled the rowdy get-togethers, ghoulish pranks, and vandalism in the cemetery. He said, "It was like *The Blair Witch Project* of New York State."

White Plains Mayor Joseph Delfino commented, "That cemetery's been there for a long time, and we definitely want to preserve that history. I'm looking forward to getting that done. The estimated cost of the monument and how it could be financed are now being examined." Sadly, after more than two decades, the monument has yet to be erected.

A few years later, additional burial records emerged naming a total of 54 people buried in the cemetery.

The list includes:

Charlotte Cowan Buckhout, Elizabeth Ann Foster Buckhout, Isaac F. Buckhout, John F. Buckhout, John Q.A. Buckhout, Nancy Buckhout.

Josephine Carpenter, Willie E. Carpenter.

(unknown first name) Cox, Emeline Cox, Harriet Cox, Mary Ann Cox, Phebe Ann Cox, Sophia Cox.

Almira Foster, Ann Odell Foster, Anne E. Foster, Elijah J. Foster, John Foster, John B. Foster, Joseph P. Foster, Jothan Foster, Mary Foster, Mary Elizabeth Marsh Foster, Matilda Foster.

George W. Marsh, John H. Marsh, Margaret Marsh, Mary Marsh, Thomas J. Marsh.

Isaac Meeks, Joseph Knapp Meeks, Mary G. Meeks, Mary L. Meeks, Moses Meeks, Solomon Meeks, William M. Meeks.

Angeline Platt, Epenetus Platt, Epenetus Platt Jr., George W. Platt, John Henry Platt, Mary Matilda Platt, Susan Platt.

Joseph Stevens.

Andrew E. Wildey, Caleb Wildey, Caleb G. Wildey, Catherine L. Wildey, Eva L. Wildey, George W. Wildey, John J. Wildey, Theodore F. Wildey.

A professional paranormal investigator checked out the site in 2008 and was spooked by hearing eerie whispers during an EVP session near Mary Buckhout's gravesite. During the investigation, the phrase "go back" was heard repeatedly. A high-grade EMF meter that recorded electromagnetic frequency also spiked dramatically near the cemetery's entrance.

The phrase "go back" has been open to interpretation. It's unclear whether it's meant as a warning to exit the grounds or as an instruction to go back in time and uncover a perhaps tragic event of the past. Digital photographs taken at the site showed what some might interpret as bright white orbs and smoke-like plasmas, commonly thought to be signs of ghostly activity.

The 2017 fictional horror movie *The Curse of Buckout Road,* starring Danny Glover and Evan Ross and filmed in Northern Ontario, depicted John F. Buckhout as a slave-owning murderer. It also showed characters known as "The Albino Twins," perhaps inspired by Moses and Solomon Meeks.

The small graveyard on a quiet woodsy road, with all of its headstones stolen or destroyed, except for one that belongs to people whose corpses may have been stolen by grave robbers, certainly has an eerie aura. While it remains open to discussion whether or not spirits haunt the burial ground or not, the removal of cemetery stones is not only a felony but a heinous act that remains uncorrected. While their gravestones may have vanished, their stories, history, and perhaps their ghostly spirits may stay on a street unlike any other: New York's scariest street, Buckout Road.

6.) EXECUTION SITE

There are numerous scary stories associated with Buckout Road. Some of them are perhaps cliché, like the urban legend about "Hook Man," where an insane criminal with a hook for a hand escaped from either a nearby prison or asylum and attacked a young couple while parked in a car. Another involves a story about a babysitter who receives multiple prank phone calls. But, when she calls the police, they trace the calls as coming from inside her house. While those urban legends sometimes associated with Buckout Road may be nothing more than spooky stories told around a campfire, one of the oldest tales related to the street has scared and intrigued people for generations.

According to local lore, just beyond the Foster / Buckhout Family Burial Ground is an execution site. The tale says that centuries ago, villagers captured three local women and burned them at the stake because they were witches. But, before the witches died, they put a curse on the land, perhaps responsible for future tragic events. Locals believe that three X's that used to appear on Buckout Road marked the location of the witches' executions.

It's unclear how this story began. Some locals swear an old newspaper reprinted an even older news article detailing the event, though the names of all three women seem lost to time. One woman, however, remains consistent: Katharine Harrison.

The focus on witch accusations in colonial America is, of course, the Salem Witch Trials. Between 1692 and 1693, over 200 individuals in Massachusetts were accused of witchcraft. Thirty were deemed guilty, nineteen of whom were executed by hanging. However, lesser known than the Salem hysteria is the Connecticut and New York witch trials decades earlier. Surprisingly, long before Westchester resident Michael Williams starred in *The Blair Witch Project*, there were accused witches in Westchester County, NY.

The New York and Connecticut state border is about ten miles from Buckout Road. Connecticut began witch trials in the 1640s, and taking an accused witch to court often took little effort. Sometimes, a single witness with a baseless claim was enough for a conviction.

In 1647, a Puritan woman named Alice Young became the first person executed for witchcraft in the 13 colonies. It remains unknown what she allegedly did that led to her grim fate. A year later, Mary Johnson of Wethersfield, CT, was convicted of witchcraft, but after locals discovered she was pregnant, they agreed to delay her hanging until 1650. After all, they were civilized and reasonable folks.

Another incident transpired a few years later in the town of Windsor in Hartford County, CT. Lydia Gilbert lived with her husband Thomas, and for a period of time, Thomas' employer, Henry Stiles, lived with them. Henry was in his early 50s, single, and a local militia member. One November afternoon in 1651, Henry and the Gilbert's neighbor Tom were doing militia training exercises. Tragedy struck after Tom's gun accidentally discharged, hitting Henry and killing him.

Tom confessed and, at trial, was found guilty of "homicide by misadventure." He was fined and ordered not to bear arms for twelve months. His father paid the fine. While this ordeal seemed to be over, the New Haven court reopened the case two years later. This time, they accused Lydia of being responsible for the shooting, causing the gun to fire through her alleged powers of witchcraft.

On November 28, 1654, Lydia was indicted and tried for "procuring the death of Henry Stiles." The panel of jurors who were residents of Windsor and knew that the court convicted Tom of killing Henry found Lydia guilty. The verdict read, "Ye party is found of witchcraft by the jury." Some historians insist she was hanged in Connecticut, while some descendants claim she managed to escape and relocate to New York.

Later that year, Lydia's 22-year-old daughter Katharine married John Harrison. She had been a servant for a local sea captain, and her new husband was the town crier of Wethersfield, CT. The couple had three children and a huge farm, which made their neighbors envious.

A few short years later, in 1666, John became sick and died unexpectedly. The 34-year-old widowed mother of three daughters was the heir to the farm and the family's money. Katharine became the wealthiest person in town. Her jealous neighbors responded by destroying her crops, injuring her farm animals, and spreading rumors that she was a witch.

The rumors spread by her neighbors led to Katharine standing trial for witchcraft. Some alleged witness accusations included claims of fortune-telling, gathering swarms of bees, damaging a borrowed hat, "rising from a cow that was not her cow", and calling another woman a "savage whore."

The court dismissed the baseless claims against Katharine, which only angered her neighbors. A few months later, they filed a petition, leading to a second trial. In October 1669, she stood trial again; this time, the court found her guilty of witchcraft.

Katharine's punishment was death by hanging. Her execution, however, was stalled. In May 1670, the court ordered her to pay a fee, be banished from Connecticut, and relocate to Westchester.

Katharine moved to Westchester with her eldest daughter, Rebekah, and Rebekah's new husband, Josiah Hunt. Josiah's father, Thomas Hunt, owned a large Westchester County farm property near The Bronx known as Hunt's Point.

Thomas Hunt eventually brought charges against Katharine, claiming she was obligated to give him property following her daughter's marriage to his son. Eventually, the judge dismissed the charges. Thomas' son responded by leaving Rebekah and quickly remarrying another woman.

That deep-dive back-story brings us back to Buckout Road, which is where it's rumored Katharine Harrison lived with her mother Lydia and daughter Rebekah until locals who thought they were witches took matters into their own hands and murdered the three women.

The popular belief is the three women were burned alive at a location on Buckout Road, later marked with three X's. The tale continues that if someone goes near the X's, "strange things will happen to you." Some residents recall hearing the urban legend in the 1970s that the witches cursed the land in response to the locals' accusations against them. During road construction in 2000, the three X's vanished.

Residents of the Buckout Road area have recalled that, during the 1950s and 60s, three infamous sisters lived on the street. While their names might be temporarily lost to time, their memory remains vivid. Known for dressing like witches resembling Margaret Hamilton's famous role in *The Wizard of Oz*, these young women allegedly placed a curse on Buckout Road! During the 1970s, one of the sisters was frequently seen near a pond on Buckout Road, dressed in full witch's garb with a cauldron. While it remains unclear if she was cooking up a potion or reheating last night's lasagna, there is undoubtedly a hunger to learn more about these fascinating individuals.

Regardless of possible witch curses, the area of Buckout Road near the 3 X's was very narrow with steep blind turns before the extensive area construction effort in 2000 to widen the street, eliminate several blind spots, and add street lights.

In 1989, a fatal accident claimed the life of a local young man named Larry Finiani while he was riding his Ninja motorcycle on Buckout Road with a helmet on. His friends recounted the story, stating the front wheel of a friend's bike accidentally hit Larry's rear wheel, sending Larry into a tree near the 3 X's. Larry's friends continue to mourn his untimely passing decades after the tragic accident.

7.)PATHUNGO'S FIERY CURSE

Surprisingly, witch curses from the 1600s aren't the first hexes rumored to plague Buckout Road with bad luck and tragedy. Dating back even further is the legend of a Native American ruler named Pathungo and his fiery curse.

As extensively detailed in *Nightmarish Neighborhood #1, The Lost Village of Kensico*, the forgotten farming village now under Kensico Reservoir, in addition to the surrounding area, including Old Orchard Street and Buckout Road, was once home to a Native American group called the Siwanoy. In 1695, a Quaker named John Harrison acquired land from the Siwanoy sachem Pathungo between Blind Brook and the Mamaroneck River.

A popular folklore version is that the agreement between Sachem Pathungo and John Harrison was for as much land as Mr. Harrison could cover in a day on horseback. The story goes that Mr. Harrison wanted to keep his feet dry, which is why the land that became the town of Harrison, NY, is the only community close to the Long Island Sound without water access.

It's believed that Pathungo and his family resided in what later became Buckout Road. Some local historians support this idea because, typically, land deeds were solely signed by the Siwanoy sachem with perhaps another member or two of the group. In the case of Harrison, however, the land deeds were also signed by Pathungo's wife, Betty, and son, Wapeto, which historians believe signifies it's where they resided.

This belief gains further credence when considering an ancient Siwanoy legend about a mysterious forest creature. The story goes that a sizeable white deer would visit the area near Buckout Road every May during a full moon. Every year, the Siwanoy searched for the mysterious white deer, believing whoever spotted it first would be rewarded with blessings and a bountiful harvest. The first confirmed sighting was by Pathungo, who named his son Wapeto, meaning "White Deer," in its honor. Centuries later, West Harrison, NY, commemorated this legend by naming a new street off Park Lane, near Buckout Road, White Deer Lane.

Some local historians also believe that a Siwanoy burial ground exists in the woods of Buckout Road. Pathungo's son Wapeto is thought to be among the buried. A cautionary tale also says that if someone steps upon his grave, they will be subjected to bad fortune.

Regrettably, a series of conflicts erupted between the Siwanoy and the settlers in the area. In a particularly notable instance, Sachem Pathungo felt that the signers of land in what later became known as Wright's Mill, and eventually Kensico, NY, had violated the terms of their agreement.

While the Native Americans didn't view land transactions the same as the settlers, Pathungo clarified that the "White Man" would not destroy the land's white wood trees, which the Siwanoy valued and utilized for making tools and canoes. For whatever reason, settlers agreed to this and then destroyed the trees and burned them as firewood.

This action angered the sachem, especially as the Siwanoy dealt with many prior conflicts with White settlers. Perhaps most notably, the 1644 massacre where Captain John Underhill and New Netherland governor Willem Kieft led an attack on a Siwanoy village, burning several hundred Native Americans to death. According to the urban legend, an angry Pathungo responded with a fiery curse on the land and its new inhabitants.

It's believed that Pathungo spent his final days on what is now known as Great Island. The off-limit island used to be a steep hill in Kensico village; however, after the creation of Kensico Reservoir, the hilltop became surrounded by Rye Lake, creating a large island. Years later, locals found large shell heaps on the island, indicating a Siwanoy presence and perhaps the burial site of Sachem Pathungo.

Centuries later, the town of Harrison erected a ceremonial Siwanoy totem pole in Silver Lake Park. Local officials and Siwanoys attended the unveiling ceremony. A few years later, the totem pole vanished without explanation.

Whether or not the potential theft and destruction of the Siwanoy totem pole reignited an ancient curse remains open to debate; however, numerous strange fires, including multiple fiery plane crashes, have plagued the area of Buckout Road, Old Orchard Street, and Great Island.

The following fifteen fires on Buckout Road over a 100-year-span have been deemed suspicious:

I.)
A fire in 1872 destroyed the home of Henry Fletcher, known locally as "Dutch Henry."

II.)
A fire destroyed an unoccupied dwelling owned by Samuel Stevens in November 1877.

III.)
A destructive fire burned the home of Samuel Thompson to the ground. The property formerly belonged to James Fitzsimmons. The fire consumed all of the building's furniture, and the occupants narrowly escaped with their lives.

IV.)
In April 1927, a description of an arson suspect was given to police by Edward McClure of Silver Lake after a Buckout Road house owned by Hugo Goulett was destroyed by fire. Mr. McClure told police, "a mysterious man slumped into a clump of bushes near the house a few minutes before it burst into flames" and that "the prowler was about 35 years old, wore a dark overcoat, dark suit, and a gray fedora hat. He was very tall and slim and of a giant stature." The pyromaniac who allegedly terrorized the area became nicknamed "The Firebug."

Later that month, Greenwich Police arrested a thirty-year-old Black man named Daniel Byhe on suspicion of the crimes. The tall man was found asleep in the woods, wearing a gray overcoat and brown suit with burn marks. A few days later, at the Harrison Police Station, Byhe was released, and all charges were dropped. Police Captain Andrew Munro told reporters, "I am convinced that man wouldn't harm anybody and is innocent of any crime."   The arson crime remains unsolved.

V.)

In 1928, an automobile was stolen from Mount Vernon and discovered on Henry Hyatt's property on Buckout Road. The car, stolen from John Portiello fifteen miles away, was destroyed by fire.

A year later, a raging fire destroyed the entire Hyatt estate. Residents watched in horror as the 150-year-old home burned rapidly to the ground as firefighters devoted their efforts to protecting five other buildings in the vicinity that got hit with sparks and burning embers caught in the wind. Despite suspicion of the fire originating via incendiary, the police made no arrests.

VI.)

Later that year, another inferno destroyed over 200 acres of land stretching from the village of Kensico to Cranberry Lake near Buckout Road. No property was damaged, but several hundred trees were killed, including trees that were once part of the tree line, which separated Siwanoy from White settlers.

VII.)

In May 1935, while returning home from work, a Stony Hill man named Theodore Price found his house on fire. With the help of his mother-in-law, Mrs. Nellie Anderson, he managed to bring his children to safety, away from the blazing structure, including his 16-month-old daughter Shirley Price.

When West Harrison firefighters arrived, they stood helplessly by, handicapped by an inadequate water supply. The blazing inferno destroyed the more than 100-year-old house and all of the family's possessions.

VIII.)

In 1941, a forest fire swept over 100 acres of wooded land. The blaze began in Silver Lake and spread into the woods on the outskirts of Buckout Road, threatening four cottages on Lake Street and a large dynamite magazine on Old Lake Street.

IX.)

In February 1942, Katherine Deutsch and her husband returned home shortly before 4 pm one afternoon to find their chicken coop on fire. Doctors at White Plains Hospital later treated Katherine for injuries she sustained extinguishing the fire of unknown origin.

X.)

Firefighters in 1954 suspected arson while putting out two fires in rapid succession that destroyed several storage buildings.

XI.)

In January 1964, Mrs. John Bannister returned home with her children shortly after midnight to find their house in flames. The house in the woods near Buckout on Stony Hill Road burned to the ground. Fire spokespeople were unable to estimate damage or pinpoint the cause of the blaze.

XII.)

In 1971, an arson fire destroyed two barns at Baldwin Farm. In 1982, vandals set the Baldwin Farmhouse on fire, destroying it.

XIII.)

In August 1972, the police deemed a series of small fires in the neighborhood as suspicious, including the 3am burning of a small red metal garage on Barnes Lane, a 3:25am blaze at a small cabin on Parks Lane, and the 3:28am burning of an old mattress on Old Lake Street near Buckout Road.

XIV.)

On February 12, 1973, Harrison Police arrested a 33-year-old arson suspect at the scene of a fire at an empty home owned by Frederick Danzinger. The fire allegedly set under the window in the foundation. It's unclear if the suspect had a motive.

Frederick Danziger graduated from Harvard in 1930 and Yale Law School in 1936 and spent his entire career with the same New York City law firm. Before his attorney days, he served as a radar intelligence officer with the Eighth Air Force during World War II.

Known as 8AF, this elite unit included the heart of America's heavy bomber force: the B-2 Spirit stealth bomber, the B-1 Lancer supersonic bomber, and the famous B-52 heavy bomber. Frederick planned and flew on multiple bombing raids against Nazi Germany.

His wife, Louise, graduated from Vassar College and served as president of the Westchester Children's Associations. She successfully led the drive to create New York's family court system. She enjoyed painting and gave her abstract art away to friends instead of offering pieces for sale.

It's unknown why anyone would want to destroy their Buckout Road house. A few years later, in 1980, the Danzigers passed away after a terrible automobile accident during a 54-mile-per-hour wind storm.

XV.)
On November 26, 1973, Harrison police found a stolen car that thieves set on fire in a wooded area off Buckout Road.

In 1974, the Westchester County Court in White Plains convicted three men of arson, including blazes set on Buckout Road. The three men were former West Harrison volunteer firefighters.

Regrettably, despite the apprehension of three local firefighters turned arsonists, strange and devastating blazes of unknown origin continued to menace the neighborhood. Past the Foster / Buckhout Family Burial Ground, where the road bends sharply to the right, sat a historic house, which, until its destruction in 2017, was one of the oldest houses in White Plains.

In 1980, the local newspaper interviewed the house's resident, a 30-year-old entrepreneur nicknamed "Tommy Trout," who ran a fish smokehouse out of the old farmhouse. According to Tom, the antiquated wood-frame house built in 1774 and located on the Heritage Trail once was a tavern and a brothel frequented by Revolutionary War soldiers.

He told *The Reporter Dispatch* that just outside the two-story, six-room house, renamed Hickory Valley Farms, people had found various artifacts, including Revolutionary War-era cannon balls, Native American arrowheads, and gold rings, believed to be wedding bands of Revolutionary War soldiers who discarded them before entering the house when it was a brothel. Despite this highly intriguing history, a mysterious fire of unknown origin burned the home to the ground in 2017.

8.) THE SLAVE REBELLION

Just two miles from the rumored Revolutionary War-era brothel, a local Quaker Meeting House on 4455 Purchase Street in West Harrison expanded from a place of prayer to a Revolutionary War-era makeshift hospital for injured soldiers. Soon after, it became the site where local Quakers gathered and made the bold decision to stand against slavery, leading to the eventual emancipation of all enslaved people in the area.

The Quakers residing along Buckout Road, under the leadership of Federick Stephens (sometimes spelled Frederick Stevens), husband of Deborah Foster, demonstrated remarkable courage and compassion. They defied the law, freeing their enslaved people before 1799, and generously donated land to the freed Blacks.

Their assistance extended to helping the former slaves construct wood-framed houses. This act of defiance and support led to the establishment of a new settlement spanning approximately 25 acres of former Quaker land along the rugged terrain around Buckout Road.

Called Stony Hill or simply The Hills, it became the first free Black community in Westchester County, which at the time included parts of The Bronx. For years, it was the county's only Black community and is thought also to have been the first Black community freed from slavery in all of New York.

Stony Hill's residents, like Cuff Brown, Jake Cox, and Morgan Stephens, embraced their newfound freedom by adapting the surnames of their former masters. Many chose to use their individual identities, like Ichabod, Prince, and Toney, while others retained their birth names, like Zingo Stout.

Despite the small size of the Stony Hill houses and the lack of modern amenities like electricity and plumbing, the community thrived. Nearly fifty houses quickly filled the area, a testament to the resilience and determination of its residents. The Butler, Johnson, Cornell, and Seymore families were among the original Stony Hill households.

While women took on the roles of house cleaners and laundresses, men found employment opportunities in carpentry and gardening. For instance, brothers Ben and Henry Hobby worked for the nearby Deutterman Ice House. Eventually, they purchased the business, showcasing the community's entrepreneurial spirit.

The eccentric Zingo Stout had a talent he exploited at Merritt's General Store. According to a *Journal News* article by Phil Reisman, *"Mr. Stout would sit on a sugar barrel and remove his hat. Then all the young men in the place would take an axe helve and strike Zingo on the top of the head with all their might, with enough force to kill an ordinary man, for three cents a crack. Zing would merely blink when he was struck and pocket the coin."*

Eventually, the Stony Hill community on Buckout Road established its own institutions, such as The Asbury Colored People's School and a church—the ancestor of the Mount Hope AME Zion that stands nearby on Lake Street. The small frame building was known as the Asbury Colored People's Church, and it stood on Buckout Road across the street from the Stephens' home, near the small schoolhouse.

The Asbury Colored People's Church became one of several religious institutions in the neighborhood, joining the nearby Quaker meetinghouse on Purchase Street and the Presbyterian Hope Chapel on Buckout Road, which was a few hundred yards west of the A.C.P.C. and where Mary Foster allegedly hanged herself.

Local legend is that the small framed Asbury Colored People's Church played a role in the Underground Railroad. A fire destroyed the church in 1916, but its original foundation still stands behind a stone wall on Buckout Road, hidden in plain sight.

Some local historians have dismissed rumors of the Underground Railroad's activities on Buckout Road because they have yet to find official documentation. This dismissal is, however, baseless. Not only would a secretive operation do its best to hide evidence, but there is documentation of multiple enslaved people escaping to the north and residing in The Hills.

One of the most respected elders of Stony Hill was "Honest John" Francis. Stolen from his native Africa sometime shortly after his birth in 1774, John spent half of his life in slavery. When he reached America, his slave master was a planter in Maryland who passed away in 1824. Knowing John was an honest man, the planter's widow quietly advised him to take the Underground Railroad to the north. She aided his escape and provided him with money for his brave journey to New York. In turn, he began using her surname, Francis, as his own.

"Honest" John Francis arrived in White Plains and made his new home in Stony Hill. Regarded as an exceptionally good person by his peers, the robust-framed man worked until he was over 90 years old.

John had many friends in Stony Hill, where he spent the rest of his days with his wife, son, and daughter. At age 92, he was insistent on exercising his right to vote, and he was conveyed three miles in a vehicle to the polls, where he voted for Rutherford B. Hayes and William Wheeler, who won the election. In 1877, John Francis passed away at age 103.

The Journal News published an article on July 17, 1999, in which writer Imran Vittachi spoke with a Harrison woman named Barbara Bush-James. Since November 1991, the 69-year-old Yonkers resident had embarked on a personal journey, working with Harrison officials to trace her lineage to multiple ancestors in Stony Hill, including Samuel Griffin, who, in the 1840s, escaped from slavery in the South and hid in nearby caves before living along Buckout Road.

A 1997 *New York Times* article by Gary Kriss also mentioned Samuel Griffin, stating he was "a Southern slave, who with the help of the Underground Railroad, escaped to Stony Hill, the rugged section of West Harrison that was home to the slaves freed by the Quakers."

Samuel Griffin became known locally as the town "doctor" due to his talent in using oil extracted from skunks he hunted to heal people, earning him the nickname "Muskrat Sam." He was an eccentric character, occasionally spotted riding around town in a rickety wagon pulled by an old horse.

It's rumored that abolitionist Frederick Douglas visited The Hills and preached at the Asbury Colored People's Church. He advocated that Blacks join Union regiments to fight the South. Perhaps inspired by his words, when the Civil War broke out in 1861, some of Stony Hill's 191 residents enlisted to serve their country.

Among them was family patriarch Alfred Seymore, who worked locally as a gardener. He enlisted with his sons James and John. They joined the 14th Rhode Island Heavy Artillery, designated as a "Colored Unit," mustered on August 28, 1863, and stationed in Louisiana.

Others who enlisted included Morgan Stephens, Simeon Anderson Tierce, Jacob Smith, John Thomas, Philip Spencer, William Brooks, Joseph Griffin, George Underhill, Benjamin, David, and Elisha Barker. According to local lore, some of these men were promised $150 to take the spots in the Connecticut Guard, replacing conscripted Greenwich citizens who were reluctant to serve as soldiers.

Eventually, the Stony Hill area extended to what is now called Stony Hill Road and a separate but connected community of freed Blacks along Westchester Ave. Unfortunately, as the area grew, so did its problems.

9.) THIRTEEN TERRIBLE TALES

A series of unfortunate events and crime rocked Stony Hill during the latter half of the 19th century.

I.) Teachers Under Attack

The police arrested a Black Stony Hill man identified only as "Purdy" for assaulting an Asbury Colored School teacher named Miss Peck. They soon after jailed another young Stony Hill man, Charles Sickles, for violently assaulting another local schoolmistress named Miss Stocum. Years later, rumors spread that Charles had murdered another Stony Hill man named Peter Beverly, but after an investigation, the police discovered it to be untrue.

II.) Arrested Hero

In July 1875, a White man named James Hyatt witnessed an intoxicated argument between a Black Stony Hill woman named Charlotte Sickles and her sister. As things escalated, Charlotte pulled a gun. Seeing this, James tackled Charlotte to prevent the shooting. As he seized her arm, the pistol discharged, firing two shots into Charlotte's legs. The police investigated and arrested James for the shooting.

III.) Independence Day Duel

The 1878 Independence Day celebration at Stony Hill took a dramatic turn when a drunken brawl erupted, drawing the attention of the local police. Amidst the chaos, they charged William Henry Barker with indecent assault, marking the beginning of a rough sequence of events.

William Brooks, a respected elder at Stony Hill and a Civil War veteran, bravely intervened, attempting to restore order and prevent the police from making any arrests. His powerful words, "It was undecidedly unconstitutional to deprive an American citizen his freedom on Independence Day," resonated with the crowd.

Mr. Brooks' words were powerful logic to Mr. Barker, who responded by flourishing a razor and a pistol to uphold liberty and the Constitution. Another local man at the scene, Thomas Tillot, responded by drawing a horse pistol and declaring Barker "too rebellious to law." After Tillot identified himself as "an assistant to the town constable," both men fired their weapons.

The violence of the brawl took its toll. Barker's shot found its mark, hitting Tillot on one of his big toes, causing a severe cut. In retaliation, Tillot's shot struck Barker on the head, inflicting a scalp wound.

A general melee broke out next, where Barker struck Constable Combs with his gun before escaping through the woods. The police arrested Mr. Brooks, charging him with interfering in police business. Mr. Tillot, though temporarily unable to walk, expressed satisfaction, claiming superior marksmanship over his adversary.

IV.) Violent Assault

In 1879, Cloyd Barker violently assaulted his father, David Barker, who had previously served in the Civil War. The police arrested Cloyd after he left his father unconscious after beating him over the head with a stone. Cloyd, who had previously served three stints in jail for various crimes, was sentenced to nine years in Sing Sing Prison. His father survived the attack but was left with a permanent eye injury.

V.) Michael Gorman

In June 1873, an Irish resident of the area, 45-year-old Michael Gorman, had gone on a several-day alcohol bending. He had been staying at the nearby Ophir Farm for a few days, where a doctor visited him and prescribed him medication to treat pneumonia.

The next morning, he collapsed while walking towards Buckout Road and died. The following day, John F. Buckhout, working as the Overseer of the Poor, interred Mr. Gorman's remains at Stony Hill's church.

VI.) O.G. Hustlers

A strange young man visited Stony Hill in the 1880s. The gentleman came around looking for work, which he eventually found from Stony Hill resident Mr. H.L. Fritz. The stranger expressed he wanted to work for money and a place to sleep. Mr. Fritz agreed, and the man, who identified himself as "J.L. Henderson," turned in for the night to prepare for a morning of work.

The next day, Fritz thought he'd pay his taxes and went to get his money to do so. He didn't find it. Fritz's savings of $25, consisting of three $5 gold pieces and a ten-dollar bill, vanished during the night, as did "J.L. Henderson."

 The police traced "J.L. Henderson" to the nearby village of Kensico, but then the trail went cold. Fritz described the thief as a 25-year-old with a light complexion, a mustache, and the letters "J.L.H." pricked into his left hand between the thumb and forefinger in colors known as Indian ink. No one other than Fritz had ever seen the alleged fugitive.

 In another instance of illegal hustling in the late 1800s, "Mr. Barker" from Stony Hill worked as a representative for the magnificent New Amsterdam Hotel. The hotel, located three miles from Buckout Road in the village of Kensico, featured 200 rooms with running water and electric lights.

The hotel needed a capable clerk to look after the guests and handle incoming funds for its opening. When "Mr. Barker" met Daniel Rooney of New York City, he knew he had found his man. They agreed on a wage of $50 per month with boarding, and because the clerk handled large amounts of money, "Mr. Barker" suggested that Rooney deposit $200. Rooney agreed and handed over the cash. The only problem was the New Amsterdam Hotel didn't exist.

Detectives investigated "Mr. Barker's" hotel address and found a small hut with no beds and two planks stretched on barrels for a dining room table. They also found a few upset elderly servants whom "Mr. Barker" had "hired" to work at the hotel. They also found "Mr. Barker" and arrested him.

VII.) Miss Kate Mack

It's unknown why a local White man named Miles Christian Hanson was inside the Stony Hill home of Kate Mack, a Black woman described as "not having a very good reputation" on Friday night, October 13, 1880. Unlucky for Miles, a well-known local named George Purdy burst into Miss Mack's house and ordered Miles to leave while drawing a pistol to his head.

Miles quietly left, but as soon as he got outside, George fired four shots at him. Fortunately for Miles, three of the shots missed. Miles took a bullet in the right leg and survived the ordeal, which landed Purdy in jail.

Perhaps unrelated, a year later, in January 1881, Kate Mack found the body of a White laborer, Daniel Farrington, dead by the roadside. It's believed he died from heart disease.

VIII.) The Green-Eyed Monster

In 1884, the police began a search for a local man named George Stevens. Nicknamed "The Green-Eyed Monster," Stevens had been fighting with his wife, leading her to move in with a man named David Barker in Stony Hill. Stevens showed up at the house and, after being denied entry, smashed out all of its windows with a rock and then fired five shots into the house while yelling threats of murder.

Three years later, two young men returning home found what they supposed was the lifeless body of a young Black man near North Broadway in White Plains. Coroner Purdy arrived at the scene to investigate. When the coroner touched the supposed corpse, it suddenly jumped to its feet, demanding to know the reason for the commotion. The coroner identified the supposed dead man as George Stevens.

IX.) Mr. Purdy

The Purdy family operated a general store on Buckout Road. In 1887, a visiting relative, William Harvey Purdy, and his wife got into an accident in Stony Hill when one of their horses shielded to the side of the road, causing their buggy to crash into a large rock.

Mrs. Purdy leaped from the busted wagon, but Mr. Purdy was caught in the reins and dragged to the foot of a hill, a distance of about 200 feet. A gentleman who happened to be in the vicinity at the time conveyed the injured man to his home. It's unclear if he recovered.

In 1889, the stoop of Purdy's Store became the site of a violent slugfest between local men "Len" Hatfield and "Dandy Pat." The police intervened, noting both amateur pugilists as "local characters."

X.) Nicholas Banker

In September 1887, Nicholas Banker, aged about 26 years, committed suicide by shooting himself through the heart. The unmarried man lived in Stony Hill near the chapel and worked as a laborer.

XI.) Francis Curren

In 1891, Francis Curren wandered from his home on Old Post Road in White Plains. The police found him sitting in a field near Stack Farm in Stony Hill without any recollection of how he got there, and they brought him home. Shortly afterward, the 70-year-old died after an attack of influenza. The local newspaper, which said he was "quite a noted character hereabouts," believes the disease caused his loss of mind.

XII.) Knife Fight

A brutal fight broke out during the Fourth of July celebrations at Stony Hill in 1891. It's unclear what exactly transpired, but Peter Beverly stabbed John Henry Barker. Both men survived the ordeal, which created a police presence at the scene.

XIII.) The Fugitive

In 1895, Eli Carpenter escaped from the Westchester County Jail in White Plains. Eli, a member of a gang known as "The Colored Rascals," had a long rap sheet beginning with a fatal shooting when he was 17 years old, killing a man named Amos June.

After Eli served his initial sentence, the police rearrested him and another "Colored Rascal" named John Smith for burglarizing a White Plains store. Eli managed to escape the jail one morning while breakfast was served by knocking down the guard, William Johnson, and climbing over a boarded fence.

The police conducted a manhunt for Eli, which went on for several months, sending searchers unsuccessfully to various parts of Westchester and nearby Connecticut. After a four-month search, two women from Stony Hill contacted the police to inquire about the reward money offered for Eli Carpenter's capture.

Sheriff John Breese and his deputies showed up at Stony Hill with rifles drawn. They questioned a local man, who told the police what house the fugitive was hiding in.

While going through some underbrush near the house the deputies were surrounding, the Sheriff's gun misfired. The loud noise confused the deputies, who all rushed to the sound of the gunshot. During the confusion, Eli came tumbling out of a pigpen outside the house. He attempted to run, but with rifles quickly pointed at him, he dropped to the ground, begging officers not to shoot. They placed Eli in a wagon and carried him back to the County Jail, to a cell specially guarded.

 In 1897, supervisors toured White Plains, inspecting several locations that had been suggested as proposed sites for a new county jail and penitentiary. Before deciding on a location in neighboring Valhalla, one of the contending sites for the jail was Holden Farm in Stony Hill.

10.)STONY HILL MURDERS

Beyond being the setting of multiple spooky urban legends and home to a history of offbeat events, Buckout Road has been the site of numerous suicides and murders. During the late 1800s, documentation has surfaced with details on at least four violent murders at Stony Hill.

I.) Baby Coombs

The screams of an infant outside his Buckout Rd home caught Charles Cowan's attention one winter afternoon in 1874. He looked outside and saw a crying child with his mother, 35-year-old Elizabeth Coombs. Known locally as Lib, the Black widow lived nearby in a Stony Hill shanty. Charles didn't think much of the incident until he mentioned it to a friend, who responded by saying that Lib didn't have a baby.

The friends became perplexed by each other's claims and investigated to see who was correct. They found Lib's footprints in the snow and followed them along the road until they reached a stone wall. When they removed a few oddly placed stones from the wall, they found the body of the concealed infant. Horrified, they contacted authorities, who arrested Elizabeth Coombs and charged her with infanticide.

An alarming news report about another Stony Hill infant broke two years later in 1876.
"A colored baby came to its death the other day in a singular manner. While leaning over a window-sill, the sash came down on its neck, choking it to death. The father of the infant is William Hardenburgh."

II.) Joseph Jackson

A poker game at Joseph Jackson's Stony Hill abode led to tragedy. On a January night in 1879, Joseph, his wife, and four guests played a few friendly hands of cards. But things quickly got strange.

A heated argument broke out between Joseph and one of his guests, William Harris. The heated words weren't about the game; Joseph was mad because he couldn't find his razor. After his wife couldn't find the missing razor, Joseph started asking William if he'd seen it, which led to William, who had no idea what he was talking about, becoming annoyed and combative.

The argument escalated, and Joseph threatened to get an ax before lunging at his guest. Several men had to pull the two apart, but that didn't last long.

Joseph grabbed a chair to swing at William like a professional wrestling villain, but William quickly countered by drawing his revolver and firing a fatal shot. The bullet entered Joseph Jackson's right cheek, passed down, and cut open the jugular vein, leaving him dead on the floor. After the shooting, William Harris escaped for parts unknown.

III.) Mr. Brown

A tragic newspaper report from 1889 stated:

"A colored man named Brown, about twenty-five years of age, was found dead in the woods in Stony Hill last Wednesday afternoon. Coroner Hopkins held an inquest, but we were unable to learn the result of the investigation."

 Further information on this incident, a potential unsolved murder, has yet to be discovered.

IV.) Elizabeth Barker

 Known throughout town as "The Boss of Stony Hill," the burly Jack Brower earned a reputation as the baddest man in town. One August night in 1884, Jack and a Stony Hill colleague, Charles Berrian, went drinking in White Plains. On their way home around 2 am, they stopped at the cottage of Elizabeth Barker.

 Elizabeth, a mulatto widow, lived in Stony Hill with her two children. Jack let himself into the house, where he found Elizabeth sitting alone in a rocking chair. The two quickly began loudly arguing about whether or not Elizabeth was involved with another local man, Thomas Tillet, whom she allegedly had spent time with earlier that evening.

Threats echoed through the summer air so loudly that Elizabeth's mother, Mrs. Eliza Cromwell, who lived next door, came to the house out of fear that Jack would hurt her daughter. Mrs. Cromwell persuaded Jack and Charles Berrian to head home.

For unknown reasons, various locals, including Charlotte Sickles, who had prior run-ins with the police, carouseled in and out of the house. Around 4:30 am, Jack and Charles returned. The noise of the pair breaking Elizabeth's locked door and forcibly entering her home caused the partially dressed woman to leap from her bed. Another loud argument began, which caught the attention of neighbor Thomas Henry Jackson, who quickly headed to the house to ensure everyone's safety.

As Thomas got to the house, the quarrel inside escalated. In the heat of the fight, Jack pulled a revolver from his coat and fired at Elizabeth as she sat on her bed. She stood up, took a few steps, and fell to the floor, dead. The bullet went straight through her heart. Her youngest child witnessed the whole tragic ordeal.

Thomas saw the shooting and tackled the drunken Jack as he and Charles tried to flee the crime scene. They wrestled for the gun, which Thomas eventually took control of. Once on his feet, Jack drew another pistol and fired several shots at Thomas. The shots all missed but took out several glass windows.

Jack and Charles disappeared into the woods as a crowd of shocked Stony Hill residents gathered at the victim's house in horror. The senseless murder led to the Stony Hill community working alongside the police to search for the fugitive.

Jack had been secretly watching the house, camouflaged from the darkness of the woods. When he saw the large crowd of armed deputies and angry neighbors, he knew they'd apprehend him if he tried to flee. He patiently waited and then proceeded in a circular route back to the house.

Entering the house, Jack stood over the body of his victim, raised a pistol to his forehead, and fired a bullet into his brain. Three witnesses watched in horror as he dropped to the floor beside the woman he murdered.

Meanwhile, the police apprehended Charles Berrian, hiding inside a woman's hut. They charged him with accessory to murder, which triggered an adverse reaction from the residents of Stony Hill, including Charles Sickles, who flourished a revolver and dared any of the police to arrest him.

Constable Barnes jumped on Mr. Sickles, who the police had previously arrested for assaulting a school teacher. After cuffing Mr. Sickles, Constable Barnes escorted him to a familiar location, the White Plains jail.

With "The Boss of Stony Hill" dead, a village elder who served in the Civil War named William Brooks stepped into the role of the neighborhood's new "boss" and restored order amongst the rowdy citizens, at least temporarily.

V.) Henrietta Hobby Barker

The police and Stony Hill's John Henry Jackson were acquainted with each other. They previously arrested him for assaulting another Stony Hill man and once came to his aid after Peter Beverly stabbed him. This time, in 1894, their interaction was because John assaulted his wife, Henrietta Hobby Barker.

 While in jail, perhaps distraught over his rocky marriage or his brother Cloyd's incarceration for violently assaulting their father with a rock, John attempted suicide by cutting his throat with a pair of scissors. He recovered, and after his release, he returned home to Stony Hill to find his wife had moved out.

 While her husband was in jail for assaulting her, Henrietta, known as "The Queen of The Hills," moved to the nearby village of Kensico, where she became a domestic helper for Justice Archer's family. Soon after his release from jail, John showed up at the Archer house brandishing a pistol, demanding his wife return home under threat of violence. Fearing for her own life and the lives of the Archer family, Henrietta returned to Stony Hill with her angry husband.

The married couple got into a heated argument on a humid Monday morning in late August 1895. Allegedly, John became angry with Henrietta for leaving her washing and their baby lying in the yard to the mercy of the sun and the flies while she went gallivanting around socializing. After they argued about this, John started walking to work, only to turn around and again see his nine-month-old child lying in the yard with flies on its face, while Henrietta was nowhere in sight.

According to witnesses, around 12:30 pm that afternoon, John grabbed his shotgun and looked for his wife, eventually finding her. A chase ensued. He stalked her movements through the woods like a predator hunting its prey. Eventually, she reached neighbor Priscilla Brooks' Stony Hill hut, who locked the door to prevent her violent husband from entering.

John broke down the door. Henrietta tried lunging through a window to escape, followed by Mrs. Brooks. John pursued after the women.

Another neighborhood woman intervened, begging John not to fire his weapon as Henrietta used Mrs. Brooks as a human shield, pleading for her life. The gun fired. The shot pierced Henrietta's lungs, leaving her dead on the ground.

John later claimed the gun misfired, though the women who witnessed the ordeal say otherwise. What happened next is perhaps even more horrifying.

After killing his wife, John calmly walked over to where she lay dead and struck her on the head several times with a spade, at the same time spitting in her face and making the remark that there were two others in the neighborhood whom he intended to kill.

The murderer remained in the vicinity for over an hour until the police finally arrived, by which point John fled into the woods which he knew so well and vanished.

The police believed John Henry Barker had crossed the State line to Connecticut and offered a $250 reward for capturing the husky 35-year-old fugitive. Over a year passed without any breaks in the case.

Finally, in late June 1896, the police received a tip from Henrietta's cousin Tilly Ackerman, who said that John was hiding just across the Hudson River in Nyack, NY.

Four officers surrounded the Nyack residence of Nathaniel Bell and quickly found John hiding inside. As they transported him back to jail in White Plains, he told the police he had traveled through the southern states but could not resist revisiting home.

John's murder trial began that December. Despite him maintaining his innocence, the court found him guilty of first-degree murder. John Henry Barker became the first man from Westchester County sentenced to execution in Sing Sing Prison's new electric chair.

On July 6, 1897, at 11:18 am, nearly two years after killing his wife, John Henry Barker was electrocuted. Sing Sing's electric chair, nicknamed Old Sparky, later became where other neighborhood murderers like Edward Haight and Albert Fish met their fate.

After his death, the court divided John's real estate, which included two lots in Stony Hill, equally amongst his four children, Georgiana, Lucy, Eliza, and John Henry Jr.

About 50 people, primarily African American women, attended John's funeral at St. Luke's Church in White Plains. The Westchester Temporary Home, which had custody of the Barker children, covered the expenses, including his burial in Stony Hill Cemetery on Buckout Road, where locals have claimed his spirit haunts.

11.)STONY HILL CEMETERY

Almost directly across the street from the site of the rumored Revolutionary War-era brothel that burned to the ground during a possible arson fire in 2017, near the former site of the Asbury Colored People Church, is a large, modern sign. Occasionally, a series of randomly placed small American flags adorn a makeshift walkway from Buckout Road a few yards into the woods towards the misspelled sign, "Stoney Hill Cemetery."

Stony Hill Cemetery, a place of intrigue, is a resting ground shrouded in mystery. It stands unique, devoid of any discovered burial records. The cemetery sprawls in various directions around the outskirts of Buckout Road towards Stony Hill Road, with small, primarily unreadable gravestones scattered throughout.

Once known as the Grand Army of the Republic (G.A.R.) Cemetery, this site holds a profound historical significance. It's the final resting place of numerous formerly enslaved people and at least 13 African American soldiers, valiant warriors who bravely fought in the Civil War. These burials were conducted in accordance with traditional African customs, with the deceased's feet facing east and marked by simple, often unadorned headstones. Among these brave souls is believed to be the only Harrison, NY resident who lost his life in the Civil War, John Brown.

In a remarkable display of community spirit, a group of Black war veterans from a White Plains V.F.W. took it upon themselves to restore the cemetery in March 1899. The site was overgrown with underbrush, poison ivy, and infested with snakes. The hidden gravestones were only accessible through faint paths that wound through the trees, over rocky slopes, and along swampy depressions.

One member of the V.F.W., Cobb Post, reportedly wanted to disinter the soldiers' remains, bring them to a clearing near Buckout Road, and erect a simple memorial with an inscription dedicated to the soldiers. Commander William White and past commander William Rogers have dreamed of the project, but it required more money than the V.F.W. could afford.

Over time, the G.A.R. Cemetery transitioned to being known as Stony Hill Cemetery. In 1939, a local man named Albert Buzzell notified the police that someone had dug up at least one of the cemetery's graves. After an investigation, the police could not determine whether or not anything or anyone had been removed from the burial plot.

Despite the population of Stony Hill dramatically decreasing by the 1940s, the rugged area surrounding the cemetery still harbored a few residents.

One of the last families of the Stony Hill community was Muriel Horton and her children. In 1960, the 42-year-old mother of four lived behind a rocky ridge about 100 feet north of Stony Hill Road. The three-room wooden shack lacked tap water, electricity, or toilet facilities.

Every day, Mrs. Horton traveled for water, drawing it from a nearby well. She lit her home with oil lamps as the sun set, casting a warm, flickering glow. Each week, she took her children to a friend's home for a bath, a small luxury they couldn't afford in their own home.

Mrs. Horton's home, a series of cramped cubicles, caught the attention of a few hikers who were shocked to see someone living in such conditions. The four Horton children slept in a seven-foot-wide, eight-foot-long bedroom. Two girls shared a bed, while the two boys shared a cot. Mrs. Horton's room, the size of a short hallway, was sandwiched between the kids' room and a kitchen with a coal-burning stove.

The 42-year-old previously worked as a nursing attendant, but she has been unable to work due to her asthma condition. Instead, she received $97.59 monthly from the Family and Child Welfare Department, of which $25 went to her monthly rent.

A few days after a local newspaper printed a story about Mrs. Horton, the community rallied together. Two local women, Louise Salvatore and Kay Magliari, took the initiative to collect groceries, money magazines, and clothing. They gathered these items by the box load and brought them to the surprised and gracious Horton family.

Nearby, one of the other final homes in Stony Hill ended in horrible tragedy.

In January 1972, two residents tragically died during a house fire that destroyed their two-story stone and wood home. Firefighters pulled the bodies of a man and a woman, burned beyond recognition from a blaze that engulfed a nearly 200-year-old home.

The police later identified the victims as cousins, 38-year-old military veteran Bernard Pease and 39-year-old Shirley Price. The latter had previously survived a nearby destructive house fire when she was a baby, saved by her father, Theodore Price.

The house, located about a thousand feet down a rutted dirt path off Buckout Rd., had no gas, electricity, or running water and was lighted with kerosene lamps and heated by wood stoves. The home previously belonged to Theodore Price, who died there a couple of years earlier, leaving the house to his daughter. Thirty firefighters fought the blaze for two and a half hours.

Fire Chief John Bambace told reporters,

"It was impossible to save anyone because the house was totally engulfed in flames. These are the first fire fatalities in the area since our department was formed in 1911. We could hardly tell the fire victims were bodies. More bodies may still lie beneath the blackened ruins."

Following the tragedy, Bambace retired as fire chief.

In 1973, a local youth named Tom Broadhurst received the Eagle Scout Award, scouting's highest honor. A Boy Scout Troop 1 member since 1968, the White Plains High School junior chose to restore a one-mile segment of Heritage Trail for his Eagle project. From Buckout Road to Silver Lake, he cleared the trail of brush and fallen trees, created a new trail through Stony Hill Cemetery, replaced fallen headstones, and cleared away the brush from ruins of an old church and an old mill which was used during the Revolutionary War for storing ammunition.

In 1999, the Westchester County Planning Department successfully added Stony Hill Cemetery to the National Register of Historic Places. Paving the way for the cemetery to receive funds for its historic preservation, it marked the first time one of Westchester's abandoned African American burial grounds gained recognition. It remains unknown how many graves the cemetery possesses, with estimates from the Westchester County Historical Society at 200. In contrast, Hal Fitzpatrick, chairman of the Stony Hill Cemetery Committee and local Mt. Zion A.M.E. church member, estimates more than double that figure.

Despite the cemetery's recognition as a historic site, the responsibility of maintaining it remains a hotly contested subject. It remains unclear whether the cemetery is rightfully owned by the town of Harrison or by White Plains' Mount Hope A.M.E. Church on Lake Street, which traces its lineage to the original Asbury Colored People's Church of Stony Hill, which started the cemetery.

As the two entities battle over the cemetery, its dilapidated condition worsens, and its history is further lost. Meanwhile, the historical cemetery has also gained a reputation for paranormal activity, with visitors reporting sightings of spheres of light and a woman in white dancing.

Known locally as "Albino Mary," local lore is that she's the apparition of a Stony Hill woman who still waits for her love to return from the Civil War. While stationed in an all-Black army unit in New Orleans during the war, Simeon Tierce wrote letters to his wife Sarah Jane, in which he promised to find a husband for her friend Mary Barker. Allegedly, Mary suffered from albinism. It's said she waited for years and even picked out a wedding dress, but her friend's husband never returned from war.

Simeon Tierce died before the war's end, and his wife Sarah Jane had already remarried by the time she filed to receive her former Simeon's army pension. However, Mary waited to find a husband until she passed away. Some area visitors have reported seeing a giant white orb floating around the cemetery believed to be her ghost. Others have even claimed to have seen the apparition of a ghostly woman in a white wedding dress roaming the cemetery, perhaps searching for her suitor.

Another ghostly phantom associated with the cemetery is a gray-haired Black man called "The Bread Man." Said to have been a local delivery man in the 1930s, some have claimed to see the appearance of truck headlights in their rearview mirror, only to have them and the truck seemingly vanish while approaching the area of the street near Stony Hill Cemetery.

In the late 1980s and early 1990s, bizarre reports surfaced that large amounts of bread and bagels would regularly appear on trees in the woods near the cemetery.

Ghost hunters are drawn to the area, seeking encounters with wandering spirits. The tales of The Bread Man and Albino Mary often take center stage on these trips, but the additional events at Stony Hill create a sense of darker, spookier energy.

Perhaps the energy left from the area's multiple murders and suicides still lingers. Stony Hill Cemetery is a location where ghost-hunting equipment like E.M.F. meters and REM pods have gone berserk, adding to the eerie atmosphere.

If two mysterious ghosts purposely roaming near a mysterious burial ground isn't eerie enough, there's more.

In Fran Capo's 2011 book *Myths and Mysteries of New York*, she included something rather interesting about Stony Hill Cemetery:

"Today, it is conjectured that the cemetery (Stony Hill) was built on top of sacred Native American burial grounds. Many ghostly figures have been spotted in the cemetery, ranging from angry, displaced Indians to Dutch children and soldiers. So much blood has been shed in the area that it's hard to tell which ghosts are the most disturbed."

The future of Stony Hill Cemetery and its preservation may be uncertain, but its historical significance is undeniable. The establishment of the Stony Hill community by local Quakers served as a beacon of inspiration for other freed Black communities in the area. This influence extended to communities along Saxon Woods Avenue and Westchester Avenue in White Plains.

Inspired by the Stony Hill community, in 1856, almost a decade before the abolishment of slavery in the United States, five acres of farmland on Saxon Woods Road near the Scarsdale and White Plains border were turned into a small neighborhood for Black families, including the family of the formerly enslaved Robert Purdy.

Over a century later, in 1978, the last of the old homes on Saxon Woods Road was demolished. At the time, the oldest living resident on the street was 80-year-old Granny Johnson.

She recalled:

"My late mother-in-law Esther Johnson gave this location to my husband, Meredith, and me for $100. We had to pay her $10 installments; the land was swampy. We built a house in 1924, should I remember; I carried more concrete than anybody.

Mother Johnson used to work for White people up on the hill, which, I think, gave her the land when they moved out sometime after the Civil War. My husband hauled coal in a truck during the Depression, but we all pitched in and mostly worked over the washboards, day and night. I heard in the old days that the Underground Railroad was in the old, old Houston house that was torn down next door."

The settlement on Westchester Avenue also started in the 1850s and drew some former residents of Stony Hill like "Muskrat Sam" Samuel Griffin. It's believed the community of about 20 wood-framed houses near St. Luke's Church, situated near a brook, was initially called Brooksville. Unfortunately, instead, the street became known by a horrible racially charged nickname.

A photograph of Mr. Griffin appears in the 1939 book *Historic White Plains* by John Roesch. The photo, which is still also displayed on White Plains Library's website, is captioned:
"MUSKRAT SAM THE GARBAGE COLLECTOR – Mayor of Blackberry Row, a Negro Settlement on Westchester Ave."

The community suffered from some instances of violence, like an 1899 gunfight between residents Josh Smith and George Dickinson and an 1891 shootout between Henry Brower and William Douglas, who worked at the Westchester County Fair cast as the racially charged "African Dodger" in a live-target shooting game. Despite the reports of violence, the White Plains settlement, derogatorily referred to as "Blackberry Row," is noted by several newspapers, including *The New York Times*, as having played a role in the Underground Railroad.

In May 1926, numerous newspaper articles emerged about a new construction project, including one from the *Daily Item*, which stated,

"To make way for the new Mamaroneck River Parkway, the Westchester County Park Commission is demolishing seven old frame houses along Westchester Avenue, known for seventy-five years past as Blackberry Row, and a station of the underground railway for fugitive slaves previous to the Civil War.

Stony Hill, a wild region, was known as a station for receiving and sheltering fugitive slaves. Concealed in the hill country hiding places, the fugitives were aided by Quakers living in Purchase and on the outskirts of White Plains. The hills formed the earliest and safest hiding place."

 In 1985, the North Castle Historical Society published a pamphlet about The Hills. Adding to the mystery of Stony Hill Cemetery, the pamphlet stated,

"This is at least one other Black graveyard in the Stony Hill area, and many of the graves are marked simply by small upright rocks, rather than inscribed headstones."

That additional cemetery's origins remain unknown.

12.) THE COTTAGE

Past the entrance of Stony Hill Cemetery once stood the magnificent estate of the renowned actress Louise Coleman. Celebrated for her character roles, Miss Coleman graced the vintage Broadway stages of New York City in a multitude of productions, including *Rose of the Rancho, Grand Army Man*, and *Warrens of Virginia*.

Unfortunately, during her retirement in the early 1930s, a tragic event unfolded at a guest cottage on her Buckout Road estate.

In June 1933, 30-year-old John DeMarco lost his wife, leaving him as a single parent to twin six-year-old girls, Evelyn and Velma. John had been out of work, leading to him and the girls moving in with his father, 72-year-old Victor DeMarco, who lived in a cottage on Miss Coleman's Buckout Road estate.

John made the decision that he wanted to put the girls up for adoption. Victor, who loved his granddaughters, happily offered to take custody of them. However, John denied his father's request and placed an advertisement in the local newspaper seeking anyone to give them a good home.

After not receiving any responses to John's ad, Victor again asked to take custody of the girls. Again, John denied the request. Victor responded by allegedly telling his son that he loved the girls so much that he'd kill himself if John took them away. The next day, John brought the girls to The Bronx to live with their aunt Mary and decided he was going to look for work in California.

According to several local newspapers, a neighbor came by later that day to visit Victor. He became concerned when nobody answered the door. When he entered the house, he found the 72-year-old hanging from a bathroom rafter, dead.

Fortunately, the twins had positive and productive lives, growing up with other family members. Velma eventually relocated to California, married, and had several children.

Twin sister Evelyn served 21 years in the Navy from 1952 to 1971 as an active duty nurse during the Korean and Vietnam Wars. During this time, she met her husband, Raymond. When she peacefully passed away in January 2022 at age 94, she was the last survivor of her immediate family, which included two brothers, WWII Army veteran Albert and U.S. Navy veteran Louis, who, after serving in the Korean War, worked as the Recreation Director at Delfino Park on Lake Street in White Plains, around the corner from Buckout Road, where, as his family put it, he was perhaps best known as "The man with the white hair and beard."

It's unclear whether John became a star in California, but a few years later, the police were back at the cottage on the Coleman estate.

A woman named Mrs. King had begun renting the cottage. One day in May 1936, she returned home to find the house ransacked. Powder, rouge, lipstick, and a jewelry box containing rings, watches, and other trinkets were missing.

Sergeant Louis Lifrier of the Harrison police department luckily found the missing items behind a nearby stone wall. Soon after, he saw the offenders, covered with powder and lipstick: a little boy and a little girl.

The two young children admitted they had entered the house around 3 pm and had been scared away by the ice man. Mrs. King declined, bringing charges against the pint-sized culprits.

13.) THE ALBINO HOUSE

Perhaps the most popularized urban legend about Buckout Road involves a young couple whose car stalls out in front of a particular house, which triggers a gruesome attack by a clan of cannibalistic albinos.

As the story goes, after the boyfriend exited the stalled-out car to check under the hood, his girlfriend heard three loud thumps hitting the car's roof. She left the vehicle to investigate and, in horror, saw her boyfriend hanging from a noose, dangling off a tree, with his feet barely touching the car's roof. The girl rushes back into the car, and she pounds on the horn three times. Moments later, the perpetrators attacked the girl, revealing themselves to be a family of cannibal albinos led by twin brothers with carving knives.

Other variations of the story include the albinos decapitating their victims and placing the severed heads in a mailbox and the albinos also being midgets. The stories of "The Albino House" have been retold so often that the details change. Moreover, the actual location of "The Albino House" varies from storyteller to storyteller, from an old white house to its neighboring small red cottage.

The creepy tale of pulling up in front of "The Albino House" and daring to honk your horn three times and then try to survive a cannibal albino clan attack gained popularity in the 1970s when it became popular for local youths to hang out in parked cars on Buckout Road and spook each other.

Back then, the road was very narrow, houses were few and far between, and there were no street lights, resulting in a scary wooded atmosphere just moments away from the hopping nightlife of bustling downtown White Plains. Many locals have shared their own stories about these activities.

One local gentleman, the son of a well-known 1950s T.V. clown, even bragged about bringing multiple dates to Buckout Road in the 1970s. Aside from notoriety as a self-proclaimed local romantic, he also proudly recounted how he and other West Harrison youth would dress up in costumes and frighten passing drivers by pretending to be ghosts. Sometimes, they'd even add props like crosses and cigarette lighters to their ghoulish weekend evening performances near trees and telephone poles adorned with various graffiti, including "Go Back," "Beware," and "Lars Was Here!"

While the details of the urban legend may be foggy, the reality is that the chance of being born albino is approximately 1 in 17,000. When two carriers of the albinism gene have a child together, that child has a one in four chance of receiving two albinism genes. Thus, a family of people with albinism is outlandish, and the idea of honking your car horn three times, resulting in being attacked by a clan of cannibal midget albinos, is absurd. While ridiculous, aspects of the urban legend have a rooted basis, perhaps scarier than the fictional tale.

On Saturday night, August 22, 1931, two guys and their girlfriends were driving home to White Plains when their vehicle experienced car trouble in front of the same white Buckout Road house popularized in the urban legend.

The car's driver, Maynard Taylor, pulled over and stepped outside to attempt motor repairs. While parked, a Chrysler coupe without its headlights turned on stealthily pulled up behind the disabled vehicle. Suddenly, two men appeared from behind Taylor's car..

A shadowy man pressed a revolver against Taylor's back while the other bandit covered Taylor's friend Ernest Greenland, who sat inside the car. "Stick up your hands and hand over all the money you've got," one of the gunmen commanded. "You dames, keep quiet," he barked at the nearly hysterical girls in the backseat, later identified as Margaret De Buono and Ella Hansen.

The gunmen stole $121 (approximately $4,000 today) from the four victims. One of the bandits then eerily remarked, "This is what depression does to you." With the revolvers still pointing at the four White Plains youths, one of the holdup men said, "Stay here for ten minutes, and don't make any noise." The pair leaped into the coupe and escaped into the darkness.

Taylor reported the holdup at the Silver Lake firehouse. The police were alerted and searched for the Chrysler coupe and the two bandits, described as being in their 30s, about 5'8" and 140 pounds. One wore a gray cap and a dark suit, and the other had a black mustache. The police searched for the robbers, who became known as The Depression Bandits.

It's believed the true story of "The Depression Bandits" may have inspired local parents to tell cautionary tales to their kids to keep them away from Buckout Road, a street that had gained a reputation for violent crimes.

In any event, it's only fitting that the most talked-about house on Buckout Road is actually the one where the Buckhout family once resided. Initially known as Old Well Farm, military captain John Quincy Adams Buckhout constructed the home in 1830. It was made of hand-hewn timber with a shingled roof and positioned against a rock ledge. The unique setup caused the wind to deflect and snowfall to blow over the house onto the front lawn. Because of the house flanking the ledge, there were no windows in the back of the first floor.

John Q.A. Buckhout lived in the sizeable 12-room homestead with his second wife, Elizabeth Ann. She was the daughter of John Foster, the original owner of Pine Tree Farm, which was just down the street. The Buckhouts had four children: Nancy, who passed away before her second birthday; Isaac, who died when he was 19; John F.; and Mary, who inherited the estate after patriarch John Q.A. Buckhout passed away in 1889, a year after his wife's passing.

According to family history, Mary Buckhout married a local man named Solomon Meeks. The couple had two young children, Isaac and Mary C. Meeks, who died young. The family is buried down the street at the Foster Buckhout Burial Ground, next to Solomon's twin brother Moses and his father, John Knapp Meeks.

For reasons unknown, over-the-top rumors of the Meeks family began. In one version, Mary Buckhout Meeks murdered her children. In another, Solomon portrayed the killer. Both versions lead to a similar creepy story where one of the parents hid the children's bodies under a floorboard of the house, leading the ghost of the other parent to forever search for the missing children, allegedly haunting the grounds of their former estate down the road to their grave site. Incidentally, the earliest gravestones targeted by vandals in the Foster Buckhout Burial Ground belonged to the Meeks family, heightening the rumors of ghostly activity.

Regardless of possible vengeful ghosts, Mary Buckhout Meeks passed away in 1897, outliving her husband by 22 years. She willed the Old Well Farm estate to a relative named Maria Meeks.

Maria's nephew, Edmund Kirkham, was born at the farm and, during the 1980s, wrote about memories there growing up in the 1910s. He recalled that his bedroom would be so cold in winter that water would freeze in a glass. He often had to sleep under four or five hand-made quilts to stay warm. To combat the cold, his family would heat bricks in the oven and then place them at the foot of their beds to act as makeshift heaters.

Edmund recalled summer chores, including fetching well water and feeding hay to their eight horses that lived at the farm. He and his older sister, Emily, enjoyed visiting their neighbors, the Klatts. They operated a berry farm and would sell them strawberries, blackberries, raspberries, and gooseberries for 2 or 3 cents a box.

Edmund recalled the changes in modern technology, citing when the family installed a water tank to collect rainwater, their purchase of a Model T Ford, and when they first had a telephone installed, the only one in town at the time for at least half a mile.

The Meeks family survived a terrible blizzard in 1918, which left them snowed in for six weeks.

In 1920, Maria decided to sell the house to help pay for Edmund and Emily's college tuition. Serendipitously, her "for sale" sign caught the attention of perhaps a surprising buyer, who passed the house while exercising.

Around the corner from Old Well Farm, the eccentric William Muldoon operated The Olympia, the nation's first health club. Muldoon, a veteran of the Civil War and a former New York City police officer, defeated Andre Christol of France in 1877 to be crowned the first World Wrestling Greco-Roman Champion. During his professional wrestling career, he became the first to add theatrics to his matches by wearing a gladiator costume to the ring.

After Muldoon retired from wrestling, he founded The Police Athletic League and helped train boxers, including famous bare-knuckle champion John Sullivan. He next pivoted to become a personal trainer, perhaps the very first personal trainer in the country.

He worked one-on-one with clients at The Olympia, which became a famed getaway destination. Known as a "health farm," Muldoon focused on enhancing his client's mental and physical health, focusing on diet improvements and exercising, often utilizing one of his inventions, the medicine ball. Some of his famous clients included Secretary of State Elihu Root, publisher Ralph Pulitzer, and famous actor John Barrymore.

A star of stage and the big screen, John Barrymore (later, Drew's grandfather), "had a reputation for heavy drinking and was drying out on Muldoon's Health Farm on Purchase Street," as Edmund Kirham recalls. "Mr. Barrymore saw our 'for sale' sign while out exercising."

John Barrymore purchased the estate later in 1920 and moved in with his romantic partner, Blanche Oelrich, who published poetry under the pseudonym of Michael Strange. To ensure their privacy, they added a high concrete wall with two antique wooden doors in front of the house.

The couple traveled extensively in Europe and often brought back various artifacts, which they integrated into the house's interior. They added four windows from a Catholic chapel in Vienna, a white Italian marble fireplace, and an entire staircase and balcony of Italian chestnut with wrought-iron filigree.

During the renovations, Edmund Kirkham recalls helping carpenters cut massive beams from the barn, which became the primary support of the balcony. Afterward, the barn looked more like a silo, which John used as an office. Later, it was reworked as a guest house.

Later, in 1920, America's first full-length horror movie, *Dr. Jekyll and Mr. Hyde*, was released to rave reviews. The silent film was shot in Westchester and starred John Barrymore in both titular roles. Perhaps on a similar level to Leonardo DiCaprio or Johnny Depp in his day, John Barrymore gained recognition as an A-list leading actor.

While living on Buckout Road, the family welcomed the birth of their daughter, Diana Barrymore. John starred in several more movies, including *The Lotus Eater* and *Sherlock Holmes*. He also starred on stage in *Clair De Lune* and *Hamlet*, featuring his sister Ethel Barrymore as Ophelia. The play ended after 101 performances, breaking the previous record for longest-running play. Locals remember he used to rehearse his lines for *Hamlet* in the backyard.

Soon after, Warner Brothers signed John to star in the films *Beau Brummel* and *The Sea Beast*. The latter became one of the studio's biggest money-makers of the year.

In 1925, John and Blanche divorced. Shortly after, John became romantically involved with his *Sea Beast* co-star, Dolores Costello. The couple had two children and multiple grandchildren, including award-winning superstar Drew Barrymore.

After John Barrymore sold his estate on 65 Buckout Road, numerous rumors emerged about its next tenants. Local lore is that famous circus little-person circus performer Admiral Dot may have been the home's next resident.

Dot, whose real was Leopold Khan, became a superstar for P.T. Barnum. At about 1/3 the size of Barnum's prior little-person stars, General Tom Thumb and Commodore Nut, Dot rose to popularity, often alongside his little-person wife Lottie, earning as much as $700 weekly throughout the country during the late 1800s.

After retiring from the circus, the couple invested their earnings in numerous properties in White Plains, including a catering hall and a hotel. The Admiral Dot Hotel in downtown White Plains became a residence of multiple circus performers until a 1911 fire destroyed it. At the time, the multi-talented Dot was a volunteer firefighter in White Plains and was amongst the brave men who fought the raging inferno that engulfed his hotel.

It's unclear where this rumor originated, but it appears baseless. Dot sadly passed away at White Plains Hospital in 1918, while the Meeks family resided in the home.

Another rumored past resident of the house is serial killer Albert Fish. Known as "The Gray Man," Fish was one of the most brutal murderers in history. The senior citizen was known to prey on children and eat their remains, including 10-year-old Grace Budd, whom Fish murdered at an abandoned house in Irvington, NY.

A suspect in ten murders, he confessed to three homicides after his arrest on December 13, 1934. He stood trial in White Plains and was executed a year later in Sing Sing Prison's electric chair.

Despite no substantiating evidence, local rumors persist that Fish resided on Buckout Road and worked locally as a house painter. While perhaps baseless, the rumors of Admiral Dot and Albert Fish living at the house may serve as the basis for the midget cannibals in "The Albino House" urban legend.

Beyond unfounded rumors of circus performers and a serial killer perhaps residing at the house, it was eventually purchased in the early 1930s by an artist named Leonard Charles Zaiss.

Born in 1892, the World War I veteran was a Second Lieutenant in the Army and was one of the first "Aeronauts," which later became the Air Force. By the mid-1920s, he became a prominent painter and sculptor. In 1925, he married Lillian Ames Chatman.

Recently divorced from horror and mystery fiction author C.A. Robbins, Lillian was an heiress coming from a prominent Boston family. She was the granddaughter of Massachusetts Governor Oliver Ames and had inherited a considerable sum from his estate.

In November 1933, Leonard and Lillian hosted a party with fellow artists at the exquisite 10-room house. Unfortunately, the evening's events unfolded like a real-life version of the board game turned movie, *Clue*.

Allegedly, during the party, Lillian referred to Leonard as "a rotter" after he visited the bedroom of a female party guest. Around 6:30 am, after a long evening of cocktails, people in the 10-room mansion heard a gunshot. The Zaiss' butler, Frank Baska, bolted through the disorderly living room to the couple's second-floor bedroom. As he reached it, he heard Lillian cry out, "Len's shot himself!"

Entering immediately, he said he found Mrs. Zaiss lying on the floor near the body of her 41-year-old husband. Frank, the butler, later told police there was no gun in the room, as he looked carefully for one.

One of the party guests, Charles Bateman, explained to officers he was walking in the spacious garden "trying to get some air" at the time, but because he is a bit deaf, he did not hear the gun shot. He did, however, hear the cry of "Len's shot himself!" and bounded up the stairs to the Zaiss' bedroom, where he picked up a pistol lying near the dead man's head and put it in his pocket.

After further questioning, the police determined someone was lying. Officers made no arrests, but the Coroner probed for more information.

Days later, the 36-year-old voluptuous blonde widow provided the Coroner with additional details. Lillian told him that Charles Bateman asked his wife, Ethyl, to dance in the nude during the party, which she happily agreed to. During her performance, Leonard remarked that he'd like to sculpt the slim, short-haired 31-year-old dancer.

Lillian explained that at around 6:30 am, Leonard left their bedroom and went into Mrs. Bateman's room. She begged her husband not to go into Ethyl's bedroom, but he did so anyway. When he returned a minute or two later, Lillian greeted him with, "Leonard, you are weak, just like your father. Whatever happens, don't let Bateman know because she loves him."

Leonard replied, "I guess I'm just no good. I'm a rotter. You are right, Lillian, I am no damned good. I am going to end it all." before taking the revolver from a dressing table and putting it to his temple. Lillian told the Coroner, "It's all my fault. I shouldn't have said what I did to him."

When questioned, Ethyl Bateman declared she was asleep from when the party ended downstairs until after the shooting. If Leonard visited her room, she didn't know it. Despite Charles earlier saying he was hanging out alone in the garden, he corroborated their stories.

When asked again about the gun, Charles said he picked up the .38 caliber revolver from the floor beside the bleeding head of his friend and placed the weapon in his pocket. "I was afraid Mrs. Zaiss might grab the gun," he said. "Later, I realized it was wrong for me to touch the gun, so I replaced it on the floor to help the police in their investigation."

Despite the perhaps odd stories given by the party goers, the police ruled Leonard's death as a suicide. Charles and Ethel Bateman were not among the dozen mourners who attended Leonard's funeral. Lillian remained living at the Buckout Road estate for several years, during which time professional piano player Charles Myers moved in as her live-in guest.

U.S. Steel advertising executive John B. Clark and his wife, Bertha, purchased Old Well Farm shortly after. In 1950, a grass fire broke out near the property. In 1953, John B. Clark died at the house following a short illness. His wife passed away in 1966, and the house again hit the market.

Doctor Tennyson Phillips and his wife Thelma purchased the house shortly after. Dr. Phillips, a 1945 graduate from New York University's School of Medicine, served as a medical officer with the U.S. Army in the jungles of the Philippines and Japan during World War II. He was recalled for a second tour with the U.S. Air Force during the Korean War. While living on Buckout Road, he served as Chief Resident at the Westchester County Medical Center and later began a solo pediatrics practice.

Thelma Phillips was born in Canada and served with the Canadian WRENS (Women's Royal Naval Service) during WWII. She and her husband enjoyed showing German shepherds and won multiple prizes at dog shows.

Despite being accomplished model citizens, local pranksters frequently targeted the Phillips' property. Beyond teenagers honking their car horns three times in front of the house at all hours of the night, people dumped garbage on their lawn, and in 1978, someone shot one of their German shepherds, leaving him crippled. Later in 1978, Thelma died following a long illness. She was only 57 years old.

Locals also harassed the Moses family, who lived in the red guest house next door, including a 1979 home invasion, where thieves stole a color television, assorted tools, and an electric heater.

Patriarch Winfield grew up in White Plains and served with the Army Signal Corps before getting a job as a commercial photographer in New York City. His wife, Agnes, worked as a telephone operator in White Plains, and their son, Michael, volunteered at the Wildcare rescue center a few doors up the street.

In the early 1980s, Glenn and Dona Tracy, a husband-and-wife team, moved their nonprofit rehabilitation center for birds of prey into a house on Buckout Road. The Wildcare Raptor Rehabilitation Sanctuary was home to nearly 100 birds, including an owl that almost starved to death, a red-tailed hawk recovering from a gunshot wound, and a rough-legged hawk hit by a Harlem Line commuter train.

The owl, Snowy, resisted being in a cage and got his own private room in the Buckout Road home dubbed "the Presidential Suite." For some time, a turkey vulture named Elizabeth took up residence in one of the bathrooms.

The Tracys acquired state and federal licenses as wildlife rehabilitators, taking in approximately 75 birds yearly. While they release the majority into the wild, about a dozen with bad injuries became permanent Wildcare residents.

Despite being bullied to the point where he legally changed his name, Michael enjoyed working with the Tracys and taking care of the injured wildlife. He edited their newsletter and once saved a wounded raccoon at the nearby SUNY Purchase College campus.

In 1984, the police found 29-year-old Michael dead in the front seat of his Dodge Dart, parked along Buckout Road. The young man, who had changed his name from Michael Moses to Michael Winfield, was found with a gun wound in his chest and a shotgun in his left hand.

In 1988, the owners of the Buckout Rd house where the Tracys operated their Wildcare operation decided to sell it. The Tracys couldn't afford to purchase the house they had been renting, so they moved their operation. Fortunately, a couple in Rhinebeck, NY, offered them the use of their 100-acre farm.

The Moses family left Buckout Road in 1989. In March of that year, a fire badly damaged the roof and a wall of the guest house. At the time, Dr. Phillips' daughter, Monica, was the home's occupant.

She was not home during the blaze. Harrison Police Officer Roger Walther said the fire "started on the outside and burned in." Another officer who lived nearby on Buckout Road, Leonard Rosa, commented there had been a flash of lightning earlier that afternoon. Rosa was the victim of a home invasion a few years prior, where a thief stole six guns, including two shotguns, like the ones used in the attack on Dr. Phillips' dog.

In the early 2000s, a young man named Tom moved into the red house.

"Sometimes, the kids drive on my property and park in the wooded area next to my house. There are signs that clearly state that this is private property. I know teens are probably just looking for a place to hang out, but don't do it here. They also leave a mess that I have to clean up

most of the time. The landlord has let the property go downhill since his wife died a few years back. His daughters have told me that the property and house once looked like a showplace. It's really a shame to see it in its current condition because it's such a nice house and property. The house once belonged to John Barrymore back in the 1920s, and no, it's not haunted. The cottage I live in has a Vermont ski cabin look to it, and it is very warm and homey. Barrymore used to practice his lines for Hamlet outside. I really like living here."

While Tom denies any ghostly activity, others believe otherwise. Claims by locals and passer-buyers have ranged from the ridiculous, like alleged albino dwarves running around the property with knives, to the slightly more intriguing, like one witness stating the apparition of a male was spotted inside 65 Buckout Road on the rafters of the home. In the exact location shortly after, a beam crashed down.

Both the main house at Old Well Farm and the red guest cottage became vacant by the mid-2000s. Local youths broke into the houses numerous times and not only damaged the property but broke all the items inside the homes and even wrote on the walls. The police did not make any arrests.

In 2008, a raging fire, labeled by firefighters as "suspicious," destroyed both houses on the Old Well Farm estate. The police made no arrests. Construction crews later demolished the burnt remains of the historic estate.

14.) YOUR STORIES

Numerous people have shared their Buckout Road experiences via my BuckoutRoad.com website and Facebook.com/BuckoutRD page. Some of those stories include the following:

I.)

"I've been there many times, and yes, the albinos are real. I don't believe they're cannibals. I was driving through there with a friend, and one albino with diamond eyes just stopped and stared at us. It was freaky, and we hit the gas pedal. I don't believe they're ghosts. I've seen ghosts in my lifetime but not there." – Robert.

II.)

"My mother told me when she moved to West Harrison she got lost on Buckout Road and wanted to stop to ask for directions. She pulled in front of a house and saw an albino midget near his mailbox. She freaked out and sped off." – Stacy.

III.)

"Some friends told me they were by the house, and some white guy came out with a shotgun" – Chris.

IV.)

"My family the Holmes, Weavers, Carpenters, Coombs, and Hobby's and all lived on and around Buckout Road for generations. The white mansion was built by John Barrymore. I went to school with Dr. Phillips' daughters in the '60s and '70s. You have no idea of the real horrors that occurred in the area of Silver Lake and Forest Lake." – Tanya.

V.)

"I had a crazy friend that once drove into the Osborne property only for us to find slaughterhouses. Not abandoned. I think I saw one of the albinos gathering his dogs" – Howie.

VI.)

"No albinos in the last 30 years I lived there. I grew up on that road. We explored those woods and cemeteries and the slaughterhouse and the underground warehouses and the bunks and caves, the old car cemetery, the skunk weed swamp, the reflection pools where the old mansion was. I saw some big snakes, bullfrogs, and snapping turtles that would take your leg off. We had the best parties out there. Middle of the day, middle of the night, rain, snow, bonfires, killer fries! I'd run the stretch of trail that went from behind my house to Silver Lake and back. I would night hike and mess with other teens partying in the woods. I'll tell you every time I got creeped out. Every time. Why I don't know. That will always be a creepy place which was my backyard. Scary as all Hell, especially that old church out there, where the

abandoned houses were. I love Buckout still though. I'll walk those trails and I'm freaked out to this day, but still, no albinos!" - Kristine.

VII.)

"I've lived in Westchester since the late 80s when I was a teenager and have gone to Buckout Road countless times seeking thrills. I've seen things appear and disappear on the road on occasion. One night a bunch of us, about 7 in our senior year in 1991, went up and walked down the driveway to what was supposed to be the albino house. 4-6 dark figures chased us in the woods that no one could get a good look at. They looked to be carrying sticks, but a few friends swore they were rifles. Any way they chased us to the end of the driveway back to our car, and we left. It's been at least 15 years since I've been there."
 - Frank.

VIII.)

"I know serial killer stuff, and Albert Fish lied there on Buckout Road. His house is creepy. It's the one with the stone gate type thing with a green wooden door in it. Anyone who doesn't think albinos live on that street knows that. One of my old teachers shared info on it. It's just sort of common knowledge." - Laura.

IX.)

"The story I remember about the Barrymore house was that someone in that house had seen a ghost on one of the rafters. Days later, the rafter broke in the spot where the ghost had been seen, killing a house resident." - Mario.

X.)

"When I was a kid in the late 1940s, my family moved from Scarsdale to an old farmhouse off Buckout Road right after it turned from Hall Avenue. I remember the cemetery which I remember being on Hall Avenue. Our house was set back about 1/5 mile on what used to be an apple farm. Our landlord was a Judge Koch who had a large estate across the road and towards Hall Avenue. He had a cider press, and we used to take apples over to be pressed into cider. At the head of our driveway was what appeared to be an old carriage house or stable. An old Black neighbor man named Bill said that his mother told him it was haunted. He claimed his mother was born with a veil over her eyes and could see spirits. I remember Revolutionary War gravestones in the woods around the house where the DAR or some org put flags in the spring. I find your site fascinating. I remember, too, that if you walked into woods parallel to Hall Avenue, you would find a swath of open ground like a road running as far as you could see. We were told it was part of the Underground Railroad for escaped slaves." – Tom

XI.)

"Nobody died there. There were no ghosts. The ghosts were and my friends. Then we'd hook up in the woods." – Joe

XII.)

The most common story going around back then, besides the Albinos, and the statue of Mary's lantern being lit or not meaning safety or danger, was the story about the White Lady. Supposedly, this was the ghost of Mary Buckhout, who had allegedly hung herself from a tree in the woods up there someplace, and now haunted the area in the form of an all white apparition. I had one friend who actually lived on Buckout

Road. She swore that her father (on several occasions) had seen the French doors leading to an outside porch that faced the woods fly open on their own, even though they had been locked. He would then see a whitish looking apparition of a woman float past him." – Laura

XIII.)

"I live in White Plains and have gone deep into the woods of Buckout. We were at the cemetery, and my girlfriend was climbing up the hill in the back of the cemetery, and she got to the top and stopped, but she didn't move and we called out to her, but she didn't move. So as I'm climbing down, everyone starts screaming and runs down the hill. They said that there were people up there, making weird low pitched, growling noises, and they were walking around each other, but their features couldn't be made out, then they all stopped and looked at my friends and girlfriend. My girlfriend said something about one of them looked like a farmer, and he was holding something. Another time we were at that cemetery, we were just hanging out there, and only half of us saw it, but there was a woman on the left part of the hill to the side/back in a white dress, and she was just staring at us, so I started to walk towards her, and she vanished in front of me, and half the people who could see it saw her vanish." –Dan

XIV.)

"In Spring 1981, I jumped on the wall of the Buckout Road graveyard, and to my horror, I saw a pit with two shovels left on the ground, a small pile of dirt, and Mary Buckhout's empty grave". – Mike

XV.)

"I drove on Buckout Road earlier today and saw someone stole Mary Buckhout's grave" – Ronnie

XVI.)

"As we were hiking out to leave, we both saw what appeared to be a globe of white light hovering in the woods about 5 feet off the ground, maybe 50 yards in front of us. It was about the size of a basketball. We actually followed it for a while, and it kept moving, always keeping about the same distance from us. After a while, it disappeared down a hill." – Tim

XVII.)

"The church was down a path. It was a wooden church with maybe five pew rows. The myth was an old lady hanged herself there. I have to ask some people about Mary, also, I studied the map, and I saw the name Fisher, something sounds right about that, like Mary Buckout was Mary Fisher, but Foster also sounds familiar". – Rick

XVIII.)

"If you walk up the old cemetery and go by the rocks, you feel something really bad. Don't go there. You'll hear growls and rocks hitting against rocks. Me and a friend sat on those very rocks, and she felt someone grab her shoulder. Later on we researched what that was all about... apparently, Mary Buckhout wanders around touching people. Creepy stuff. After they tore down the old barn, some friends were able to get pictures of vivid light ghosts." – Jason

XIX.)

"I am 48 years old and lived on Lake Street, my best friends lived there, the haunted white mansion that's in the process of being torn down, stories of grave robbers we saw many plots dug up coffins opened, even have the heritage trail that passes through Buckout ...was used by the Indians the pilgrims, intense real...witches, ghosts...man do I have stories. I live up in Orange County now. Buckout, Lake Street, and Park Lane all held maybe 10 houses on them. Park Lane that backs up to Buckout used to house an abandoned farm slaughterhouse of pigs. The main house was deep within the woods, beautiful, now garbage mc mansions reside there... history all lost, all torn down for garbage."
 - Barbara

XX.)

"One night I was driving there, and it looked as if there was this drop off, like it was the end of the earth, and I totally freaked out. I started screaming how I didn't wanna drive down further. Everyone was persistent in me to keep going and I did little bit further and the car got stuck and I swear to God I heard voices call out to us. Then a second time we drove out there and kept on that path in the day time and came up to this old eerie mansion of a house. No cars, no nothing were up there. It seemed like these faces were peering out the windows at us. I took back to the car it was a long time before I couldn't go through there again. Eric, it freaked the hell out of me." – Sara

XXI.) Rick's Party In The Woods

I can remember being alone, on a cold winter night, wind blowing furiously, the trees bending in anger, as I walked alone past that graveyard on my way to where the mansion was, thinking I hear voices of my boys partying and getting closer, and not hearing anything when I got to the swimming pool which was then just a filled-in hole in 1985. We partied just beyond the pool at an outdoor fire place made of cement with a semicircular bench arrangement. I remember when I was young, before we starting smashing out the streetlights on Buckout in my teens, there were these really creepy lights, like little bare bulbs hung underneath tin plate shaped covers, which gave off an almost dim, useless glow. My buddy Derrick was the ONLY white kid that lived in the White Plains projects. He was a good friend of mine and came to the woods and my moms' house on Buckout to escape the city of White Plains (and I went to his place for some kick ass project parties). He would often take groups of young kids that lived in the White Plains projects to explore the woods with him and teach the nature and show them the abandoned 'town' in the woods. That well known we had in Buckout woods, well, Derrick was the frigging coordinator and MASTER planner. All-day long, we had 3 kegs, 12 cases of liquor, and 2 cases of pink champagne and other miscellaneous party supplies dropped off by the house, a'hem... ANYWAY THEN we had to get ALL that ALL the way into the woods. Getting kegs in there was always a B!.. We had van passenger transport from a remote location as not to park too many cars on the road for suspicion purposes. But the cops monitored the cab frequency, and at least 8 full cabs were called to my address.

(And my father's best friend was a cab driver, so my dad was an unexpected and unwelcomed guest later that evening). The cops also got a hold of maps and a flyer about it. They stopped about 40 of Derrick's boys from the projects walking up Buckout. The cops sat outside with loudspeakers trying to coerce kids out to no avail. But getting people out was the best. I smuggled people up through other trails and out at different locations when they wanted to leave. Or up the trail, snuck across the dark street, in my back door and out my main door --which is in site of the police. 50 kids, at 1 time or another in the evening, walked out the front door of a house that had no lights on, NO noise, and appeared to be, and was empty. They got into a waiting car, their own car, or a cab. From the road, it sounded like there were 100 people way in the woods ...the din was sick sounding, and we had 3 boom boxes handcuffed to trees surrounding the party for good party music. Needless to say, the cops were not even thinking about going IN there. HAHAHAHA ...From the road you could NOT figure what the hell was going on in there!!! We are way back there you know. The day after we had to go in and look for passer outers and found a few. We cleaned a lot up. No canned beer was aloud so we didn't have to clean that up. WE put out the 3 large bonfires ...THENN the cops show

up with dogs. ALL they found was one passed out dirty kid, unharmed. Here's the casualties: 1 s burn from a guy, idiot falling into a fire (they carried him the HELL out of there and then carried on with the PAR TAY.) 1 case of Limes disease, 1 case of chick passed out in someone's front yard 1/2 naked... let's see what else...OHHH We couldn't wake up this skinhead in his car about 7 am....so the other skins lit a pack of firecrackers under him and he jumped up from the back-seat and BASHED his head so bad into the roof (ooof I saw that and it sucked) He got out and beat up one of the other guys pretty good, and at least 100 terrible hangovers. The cops picked up 2 kids, 1 puked in the cop car, and the other was some cops kid, so they dropped them off 2 miles down the road. I don't believe anyone was ever arrested. SO, my mom comes back from vacation, and we had to tell her what happened--well, not EXACTLY what happened. We downscaled that BIGTIME. -- But it was gonna get back anyhow....I was about 16 and my brother about 18 I guess. ....So her cop friend calls her up, and it went a little something like this: MOM: Look, I told you the kids were gonna have a little party, what was with the Calvary. COP: That little party was probably the biggest party ever pulled off in the history of White Plains.

pauseeeeeeeeeeeeeeeeeeeeeeeeeeeeeeeeeeeeeeeeeeeeeeeeeeeeeeeeeeee MOM: WHAT!? First time I go away it ten years and those little mother F'ers did WHAT!!!?? It would be almost impossible to get away with this shit these days. I did say almost" - R

XXII.)

Foster family descendent Joe Kelly shared some handwritten genealogy written by his relative Elvira T Stephens Murphy, known as Vera:

"May 8, 1972. Our Old Cemetery on Hall Avenue:
I have John Foster's will. He willed to our family on August 29, 1841,
this cemetery forever and forever. John Foster died September 10,
1841. He and his wife are buried in the cemetery. Deborah Foster
Stephens was his daughter. (Deborah is) Our great, great,
grandmother, she is buried with Frederick Stephens. Joseph Stephens,
born April 9, 1821, died August 26, 1897, son of Frederick and
Deborah. He is on the right side as you go in the old cemetery with his
family.
Starting at the gate arc, the graves of William Meeks, Moses Meeks,
Mary L. Meeks, Isaac Meeks, Ephentus Platt, Sarah Foster, John
Quincy Adams Buckout. Caleb Wildey died 1948. There is, I believe,
about fifty people in this cemetery and still can be used. Caleb Wildey
married a Buckhout uncle to Al Cerak & his family

Headstones – vandals took them and threw them throughout the county.
I had the police put them on Dave Baldwin's farm. I have told them the
City of White Plains they do not belong to them, and I have their reply
regarding the headstones. As you know, Dave Baldwin is in our family
on the Foster side."

15.) INCIDENTS

In addition to the various spooks, horrors, and tragedies of Buckout Road, the street has a history of odd incidents and strange crimes. Some are perhaps borderline humorous like the two toddlers stealing makeup from the Coleman estate in 1936. Others, however, are dangerous, scary, tragic, and, more often than not, just bizarre.

Bird theft increased in 1880, including one incident when the police arrested Delancey Barker and Foster Watson in Stony Hill for stealing several ducks and chickens from a nearby farmer's coupe. The local bandits defended their actions by saying they wanted to bring the birds to their church's upcoming donation event.

Another Stony Hill man, Abraham E. Brown, spent nearly a year in jail for stealing chickens from White Plains farmer Wilson Tibbits. After his release, Abraham burglarized a home in Port Chester. The police quickly apprehended Abraham, who paid for the break-in with a ten-year sentence. The judge took no pity on Abraham, known locally as "One-Armed Abe," as he was missing an arm.

In 1905, an unknown burglar broke into a home and stole two beehives.

In perhaps White Plains' first case of personal injury fraud, 80-year-old Stony Hill peddler John Parker claimed a wagon struck him in 1913, causing him an injury and preventing him from working. Luckily, Mr. Parker miraculously recovered from the incident, just as he had from several other similar prior incidents. The next day, he resumed selling lead pencils for loose change.

In August 1925, a drunken brawl between Stony Hill residents at a picnic led to three arrests for assault. It's unclear what transpired or who "won" the fight, but Judge Sullivan awarded thirty-day jail sentences to the two main participants and a 60-day sentence to 31-year-old female participant Annie Nichols, who he described as a "dusky amazon."

The police arrested WWI veteran Ernest Hobby of Stony Hill in 1927 for driving a stolen car. Years later, a Harrison police officer found members of the Hobby family, including a father, mother, two small children, and a baby, living inside a sedan parked on Stony Hill Road.

In 1931, a wrecking crew from a local garage, LaVigna's, had the six-hour task of tugging a 1928 Cadillac coupe out of a swamp in the dense woods of Stony Hill. The stolen car was discovered by a boy named Charles Buzzel, who was playing in the woods.

Later that year, police arrested Charles' brother, Vincent Buzell, of Buckout Road, who admitted to robbing four White Plains stores and stealing eight automobiles, leaving them abandoned in the woods.

In May 1933, three people from Yonkers forcibly kidnapped a man in North Tarrytown, robbed him of $21, and dumped him on Buckout Road. After arresting the three crooks, the police believe the 22-year-old woman bandit lured the unsuspecting victim into her car.

The police were drawn to Buckout Road on a hot summer day in July 1936 after well-known Stony Hill resident Charles Sutton fired a shotgun in the air, allegedly to scare another man, Carl Fedlia, after he refused to spend 25 cents for a glass of cider. The police had become acquainted with Mr. Sutton after numerous disturbances at his home, which often involved a woman half his age named Irene, sometimes resulting in charges of disorderly conduct. Irene's rap sheet included a stint in an Albany jail following her conviction as a jewel thief.

During the summer of 1939, a handyman named Earl Ackerly, who lived on Buckout Road reported a prowler to the police. Earl said he witnessed a man bothering a young girl in the nearby woods. Later that summer, the police arrested a gang of five men who admitted to a string of summer bungalow robberies near Rye Lake. The arrested thieves included two handymen who lived on Buckout Road, Walter Phillips and Earl Ackerly.

Years later, a publically intoxicated Earl allegedly tried forcibly entering a West Harrison woman's car. When the police arrived, the tipsy Earl said the woman ran him over.

In 1940, Silver Lake constable Arthur Sloane turned over several sticks of dynamite and a can of black powder to the Harrison police. Sloane got the explosives after new homeowners discovered them while cleaning out their new house on Buckout Road.

After a police chase in July 1940, authorities apprehended 18-year-old Buckout Road resident Melvin Solomon. The son of a preacher man confessed to burglarizing multiple Westchester gas stations. He also admitted to selling stolen car parts. After searching his vehicle, detectives found tires, fog lights, and a radio stolen from a local Texaco station.

In 1942, the local newspapers printed photos of three men wanted by the FBI, graduates of the "German Nazi Sabotage School." Later that Sunday, a Buckout Road woman named Helen MacCallun reported that one of the FBI's Most Wanted had accosted her. It's unclear if it was a case of mistaken identity or not.

In 1951, the police arrested 23-year-old Raymond Price for allegedly being found with "obscene pamphlets."

The police arrested John Field numerous times. Once, the Buckout Road man charged his car into a telephone pole while driving intoxicated and fleeing the scene. Another time, he allegedly ran over and killed a dog.

In 1960, Mrs. Henry Borris reported that her new mink coat was missing. Also missing was her new 20-year-old maid.

In 1967, the police discovered the creation of an "automobile graveyard" consisting of at least 20 demolished cars. The juvenile culprits included two West Harrison 15-year-olds. The stockpile of stripped cars was discovered after a neighbor saw smoke after the kids set one of the cars on fire. According to rumors, locals held makeshift demolition derby races in the woods.

Later in 1967, a highway department employee cleaning out ditches on adjacent Old Orchard Street and Buckout Road found shoeboxes full of suspicious items that he turned in to the police. The boxes contained several hundred pills and 39 $10 packages of marijuana.

The police quickly realized it was a drug pick-up situation and arranged a sting. Off-duty officers hid behind trees near the replanted empty shoeboxes. A Jaguar pulled up, and its two occupants leaped out and checked behind a stone wall for the first box. When the police emerged, the drug dealers jumped back in the car and hit the officer as they sped off.

Two years later, in a perhaps related incident, Ronald Pryor's German shepherd, Cyclone, surprised his 27-year-old master when he came trotting into their Buckout Road home with a bank money bag. Inside were nine disposable needles, syringes, 18 pills, 21 amphetamines, and other assorted paraphernalia. It's unclear where Cyclone found the stash.

In 1973, while walking on the Heritage Trail, Mr. and Mrs. Joerg of West Harrison discovered the body of a woman in a seated position next to the open door of a small truck. The police identified her as 47-year-old Mary M. Chernin of Ramapo, NY, who her husband had reported missing. Police said her vehicle had struck a tree in the woods.

In 1976, someone called the Harrison Police Department to report a dead body in the woods. When the police arrived on Buckout Road, they discovered the "body" consisting of white pants and a blue shirt stuffed with newspapers and decorated with ketchup.

In 1978, the police arrested two West Harrison men, charged with picking up an 18-year-old woman in New Rochelle, driving her to Buckout Road, and raping her.

A White Plains man left his construction job at a Buckout Road job site for about an hour one afternoon in October 1979. Instead of running out for a hot dog from The Little Spot, he pulled off a burglary. On his way back to the construction site, he drove his car into a ditch.

When Harrison police came to help him, they spotted office machines and sporting equipment in the backseat, matching the description of stolen items reported a few moments prior from the Carter family on Buckout Rd.

By 1980, residents cited vandalism and numerous burglaries, like the dangerous one in 1972 when a robber broke into a police officer's house on Buckout Road and stole multiple firearms, as evidence of a need for protection.

Another concern for residents was the increased number of hunters in wooded areas where people would enjoy nature. The town of Harrison tackled the concern by posting multiple signs that read "No Trespassing."

On July 4th weekend, 1990, George Coombs reported that he heard a loud explosion around midnight. When he went outside, his mailbox had been blown apart by firecrackers. The 82-year-old fourth-generation Buckout Road resident who served with the U.S. Army in World War II worked as a Westchester County Highway Department foreman for 35 years and sang in the Lake Street Full Gospel Church didn't understand why anyone would want to destroy his mailbox.

A few years later, an explosive destroyed another nearby mailbox on Buckout Road, resulting in a presence from the Westchester County Bomb Squad.

Perhaps the most violent and tragic incident began to unfold in 1995 when a 17-year-old girl invited her ex-boyfriend to a party. However, instead of going to a party, she picked up the young man at his Mount Vernon home with two other teenagers and drove him out to Buckout Road. Then, they beat her ex-boyfriend with their fists, took his wallet and his clothes, leaving him naked on the street. The residents of a nearby home called the police when the beaten young man knocked on their door seeking help.

A similar incident occurred shortly after when a 19-year-old Harrison man was lured out at around 3 am and then beaten by four teens. The victim also knew the 17-year-old girl responsible for the Buckout Road kidnapping and attack. Shortly after, the police arrested her, and charged her with second-degree robbery.

After her mother posted her $7,500 bail, the police released the 17-year-old girl. However, after her mom refused to pay an additional

$10,000 to bail out her teenage boyfriend, who orchestrated the violent attacks, the 17-year-old threatened her mom with a knife, leading to the police arresting her again and placing her in jail.

After refusing to take prescription medicine and discovering that she'd be facing a prison term of between two and four and a half years, she grew increasingly upset. In May 1996, the 17-year-old hanged herself with a bed sheet inside her Westchester County Jail cell.

Fortunately, the most recent memorable incident on Buckout Road was far less tragic. In 2020, film crews set up at a Buckout Road home to shoot an episode of the HBO drama mystery thriller series *The Flight Attendant*. The critically acclaimed series, starring Kaley Cuoco of *Big Bang Theory* fame, received numerous nominations and won multiple awards.

16.) THE NORDA EXPERIMENTAL FARM

As you venture along Buckout Road, past the infamous "Albino House," and the charming new homes, you'll come across an intriguing intersection with Carriage Hill Drive. In the 1970s and 1980s, this spot was not just a culdesac with lavish homes but a driveway leading to a solitary house shrouded by a dense forest.

The house at the end of the long driveway was more than just a structure. It was a part of local folklore, a place of mystery and intrigue. A chilling tale emerged in the 1970s when a babysitter in the house was tormented by prank phone calls, leading to a police investigation. The shocking revelation was that the calls were coming from within the home. This enigmatic house even allegedly served as the inspiration for a horror film. In the early 2000s, the house underwent a transformation, becoming the office of a local fuel and oil company.

Whispers circulated about century-old neckties, supposedly belonging to former tenants, mysteriously hanging on attic doorknobs. In 2000, tenants left the house, which was soon demolished, leaving behind a trail of unanswered questions, adding to the mystery of the place.

Similarly, other modern culdesacs off Buckout Road, like Castle Brooke Road and Golden Pond Road, have been added in recent decades. The latter, formerly referred to locally as "Lover's Lane," was a rumored hangout for teens in the 1970s and 80s before lavish new homes sprouted up.

Construction began in 2023 on a new culdesac off Buckout Road, which, like the others, also used to be woods. Luxury homes on the new road, Hayden Lane, started hitting the market in 2024.

Decades ago, Buckout Road's landscape was a stark contrast to its current state. Beyond the thick woods, lack of street lights, and clusters of Stony Hill bungalows instead of mansions, the street was home to multiple farms, including a vast one known as Norda.

Dr. Herman Joseph Kohl was born in Germany and moved to New York in 1911, shortly after obtaining a PhD in chemistry from Heidelberg University. He became the founder and board chairman of Norda Essential Oil and Chemical Company, a manufacturer of flavors and perfumery.

When Dr. Kohl moved to Buckout Rd., he purchased a massive estate that took up a large chunk of the street and extended to adjacent Park Lane. Situated near The Anderson Farm on Buckout Road and the vast fruit orchards of Frank Park's 200-acre Hillside Farms on Park Lane, Dr. Kohl transformed his estate into The Norda Experimental Farm.

Unfortunately, in 1939, the estate became the first targeted robbery of the local gang of robbers led by handymen Earl Ackerly and Walter

Phillips. The group of five crooks busted into Herman Kohl's house and stole ten bottles of cider champagne. While it remains unclear if they got to celebrate or not before the police arrested them moments later, they were out of jail sooner than later and back to committing numerous robberies on the street. Unfortunately, a much more gruesome situation unfolded on the Norda property year later.

What began as a routine Monday morning for White Plains milk truck driver John Sala took a turn after he noticed something peculiar at Norda around 10 am. Protruding from behind a stone wall of the massive estate were human legs. Upon closer inspection, a horrified Sala discovered the body of a young Black girl in a maid's uniform.

A close-range shotgun blast had blown off part of her upper head and face. Mr. Sala immediately notified the police, who found a shotgun shell near the body.

Her bloody, rumpled clothing gave evidence of a struggle, and a trail of bloodstains and footprints led to the belief her slayer dragged her to Kohl's property after the fatal shooting occurred about nine feet away on Buckout Road.

The young woman's maid uniform helped investigators identify her as 26-year-old Lucille Johnson of Greenburgh, NY. Lucille worked as a maid in White Plains and was the common-law wife of Charles Wynn of White Plains.

The police wanted to inform the victim's husband of the discovery. When they arrived at his place of employment, St. James Church in

White Plains, where he worked as a janitor, they discovered his body, dead on the floor.

 Near his body, the police found a sawed-off shotgun. They learned the couple had left their prior marriage partners for each other. While uncertain what triggered the fatal quarrel, they ruled the situation a murder/suicide.

 Fortunately, things remained quiet at the Kohl estate until late July 1949, when a strange fire, notorious on Buckout Road, broke out. The blaze engulfed a 75-by-50-foot single-story wooden warehouse, destroying its contents, including an oil drum, a boat, and two tons of peanut shells.

 In 1950, Joseph Pryor, who lived on the street and worked as the superintendent of Norda Experimental Farms, notified police that someone was shooting guns in a nearby wooded area. A few months later, in early 1951, farm employee Louis Vitali reported that something or someone triggered the farm's burglar alarm.

 Luckily, in both instances, no damage occurred. In 1959, however, six large Black Angus escaped from the farm and led police on a wild chase. Over one hundred officers tried to apprehend the escaped cattle for three months.

 The runaway bulls weighed a menacing 1,500 pounds each and were often destructive. WWII veteran Colonel J.R. Elyacher, who served under General Dwight Eisenhower as commanding officer of Military

Intelligence, watched helplessly as the herd destroyed his Buckout Road cornfields.

Locals often spotted the herd grazing near a pond on the Manhattanville College campus. Westchester County officials slipped tranquilized pills into piles of hay near the site to make the cattle tired, though that did not work.

Officials used airplanes and helicopters to track the herd, which eventually chaotically crossed the heavily trafficked Hutchinson River Parkway. A judge summoned Joseph Pryor to appear in City Court to face the charge of an "agricultural law violation."

In March 1959, Prior, along with Westchester County Jail warden Maynard Allen and Deputy Sheriff Paul Black, tracked the herd near the campus of SUNY Purchase. Eventually, under the orders of Sheriff Black, Harrison police officers killed the cattle with rifles. The cattle were then bled and strung up in a Norda barn and eventually turned into several thousand pounds of hamburger meat.

Two years later, in 1961, five pigs escaped the Norda farm. Fortunately, a local woman discovered the pigs on her front lawn near Cranberry Lake later that day. In 1963, vandals broke the lock on the farm's gate. The intruders broke into the pigpen, chased the pigs, and broke property in the main barn. Before exiting, they stole a two-foot-high bronze statue of Moses.

Soon after, spooky stories about alleged "pig slaughterhouses" on the farm began circulating through town. Urban legends began that various shady characters reminiscent of those found in the classic horror film *The Texas Chainsaw Massacre* were brutally slaying pigs on Buckout Road. Despite teens rumored to dare one another to explore the pig slaughterhouses at night, no photographic evidence of the rumored site has emerged.

In 1970, firefighters fought a blaze at Norda Farm, which destroyed a shack. During the two hours firefighters battled the fire, a vehicle involved in a high-speed chase with police that originated at nearby Westchester County Airport ended when it struck the fire truck.

Thieves broke into Norda in 1982, stealing numerous items and destroying a grain house. The farm closed shortly after.

In addition to the Norda Experimental Farm and previously discussed Wildcare Raptor Sanctuary, animals have always been a part of Buckout Road's history and charm.

In the 1960s, former Broadway actress Bette Butterworth operated a menagerie of various animals on her 14-acre Buckout Road estate. Her collection, which began with a few dozen cats followed by a pair of goats who provided milk for the cats, grew to include collies, hens, ducks, rabbits, and pigs. Local children would look forward to interacting with her tame animals on school field trips, especially members of her "zoo" like Kit-Top Joan and her kittens, who appeared on the hit television show *Captain Kangaroo*.

A few doors away at Fieldstone Farm, Sue Kammell operated Pet Rescue, an animal shelter for dogs. In 1986, West Harrison determined the refuge violated zoning codes with its fenced-in kennels and issued an eviction notice.

Sue fought the order, stating she was legally entitled to have the number of dogs she did on the 18-acre property, which has three houses. She found homes for most of the shelter's dozen dogs within days of the newspapers reporting the eviction notice.

Horror struck another Buckout Road resident in 1990. After discovering a broken fence and tracks left by Davey and Gordon, her two 100-pound male lambs, owner Christina Hughes told police that an intruder may have broken into the closed barn during the night, where her lambs were sleeping like, well, lambs.

While farm animals are a rare sight on Buckout Road these days, the area is still home to multiple wild animals. Perhaps it may be good to remind people who enjoy wandering in the woods looking for ghosts or alleged remains of sinister slaughterhouses that, in addition to the peaceful deer and rabbits that inhabit the area, locals in recent years have seen bobcats, coyotes, various snakes, and gigantic black bears.

17.) THE NEW HORROR

Named after Hillside Park founder Roger Park, Park Lane is a nearby street that intersects with Buckout Road. The large Norda Experimental Farm property extended from Buckout Road onto Park Lane, with entrances on both streets.

During the autumn of 1931, a pair of criminals, August Million and his brother Willhelm, terrorized wealthy residents of Westchester for more than eight weeks. Known as "The Motorcycle Bandits," the pair committed multiple robberies until finally being apprehended by Harrison police officer John Lieb.

Officer Lieb saw the pair speeding down Old Lake Street on a motorcycle when he engaged in pursuit, resulting in their arrest on Park Lane. The judge sentenced the pair to 20-40 years in Sing Sing.

A few years later, a strange news report emerged stating that a man named "William Million" escaped from a New York prison. Police believed he may actually be a different man, Roger "Scarface" Million, the head of a Paris gang wanted in connection with at least ten murders. After much speculation, it proved to be a case of mistaken identity.

In November 1946, Harrison police officer John Lieb was found dead of a bullet wound in a parked car on Park Lane. Medical Examiner Amos Squire pronounced the death of the 42-year-old to be a suicide.

By the 1950s, the residents of Buckout Road feared something new that was much more frightening than rumors of cannibal albinos: the threat of nuclear war. As the Cold War between the United States and Russia heated up, so did the fear of a nuclear weapon exploding in the area of New York City.

Scary scenarios of nuclear incineration dominated the public's imagination. In late 1955, the U.S. government spent $4 million to construct a missile base to protect the metro New York area from a foreign attack. The defense of New York City relied on this new missile base built on Park Lane, just near one of the entrances to the Norda Experimental Farm.

The Soviet nuclear program sped ahead in the mid-1950s, and the prospects that an annihilating strike would turn Westchester into a glowing heap of rubble became alarmingly real. The paranoia over an enemy attack began during the Korean War, prompting some residents to envision the menace in their backyards.

The all-out fear reached a high on November 26, 1955, when *The Reporter Dispatch* released a special "Civil Defense Test Edition" of its newspaper. The horrible headline read, "SILVER LAKE HIT BY ATOM BOMB, 500 IN CITY KILLED, 3,200 INJURED," with a photograph of a mushroom cloud over West Harrison. The article continued with gruesome details, written as if an atomic blast had actually taken place in West Harrison and what may have happened.

As part of the preparation drill, more than 1,000 White Plains Civil Defense workers were mobilized to cope with the simulated atomic bomb attack. According to the simulation, "the bomb exploded at an altitude of 3,000 feet over the northwest corner of Silver Lake Park near the White Plains reservoirs on Old Orchard Street." Part of the drill included all vehicles pulled over to the curb for about ten minutes while pedestrians on the streets took shelter.

The fearful public responded to the ongoing atomic bomb threat with a craze for building underground shelters in their backyards. Twenty-inch-thick concrete bunkers were lined with heavy metal to ward off lethal gamma rays. The bomb shelters were stocked with canned meats, water tanks, and a few amenities inside so a suburban family could, theoretically, ride out the nuclear apocalypse in modest comfort.

Over one hundred enlisted men, six officers, and two warrant officers staffed the new defense site on Park Lane. Commanded by Captain John W. Feiger, approximately thirty Nike Ajax Missiles armed the location, about half a mile from Buckout Road.

Each missile was about twenty feet long and about one foot in diameter. When launched to intercept an incoming enemy weapon, the missile would be attached to a 15-foot booster, accelerating the projectile to supersonic speed before separating from it a few seconds later. The Army described the installation as safe as a gas station and as essential to community security as police and fire departments.

The base occupied nearly 40 acres. About seven acres at the top of one hill served the control area, with its computer radars and associated remote control equipment, barracks, mess hall, recreation hall, offices, and supply room. Approximately 33 acres at the top of a distant hill was the launching site with fueling areas, underground Nike warehouses, and launching racks. When fully operational, the base was active 24/7, with patrols on the perimeters.

On May 22, 1958, an accidental explosion of a Nike Ajax missile at a base in Sandy Hook, NJ, detonated seven other missiles lined up in the base. The blasts blew out the house windows miles away, and the news widely reported the disaster. The disaster caused the public of metro New York to fear bombs from Russia and now also explosions from their homeland defenses.

Despite the increased fear around town, residents on Park Lane shockingly expressed a different view. Mrs. Edwin Fisher, who lived across the street from the base for over a year, told reporters, "When your time comes, there is nothing you can do about it, so why worry?" Mrs. Stanley Bang, who lived 100 yards from the firing range, added, "An accident can happen anywhere. I see the Nikes when they're raised, but it doesn't bother me."

Fortunately, no blasts occurred in Westchester, and in 1960, the New York Army National Guard took over the operation of the ground-to-air firing base from the U.S. Army. This move coincided with the arrest of an army private at the base. The police arrested Private Holt after accusations of attacking a Yonkers woman. After admission, he was charged with rape.

The New York Army National Guard abandoned the missile base a few years later. Around 1965, newspapers reported that the federal government had agreed to turn over a 6.4-acre section of the former missile site to the Westchester Board of Cooperative Educational Services. The site's intended repurposed use was a school for the special education of mentally and physically disabled children. For whatever reason, the plan never moved forward.

Around 1969, the town of Harrison purchased the vacant site, which had become highly vandalized. Officials filled 30-foot-deep bunkers with water to defer future break-ins.

Harrison officials told taxpayers they'd convert the 40-acre site into a public recreational area. Some proposed uses included sledding, ice skating, bicycle paths, a picnic area, tennis courts, a football field, and a golf course. The underground area, lined by four-foot concrete walls, was considered for a rifle range or a bowling alley. Proposed uses for the concrete asphalt area included a model plane launching site and a mini car racing area.

Despite Harrison's dwindling open space and the increased demands for expanded recreational facilities, over fifty years after Harrison purchased the site, nothing was ever built.

The town instead repurposed the site as a rifle range in the 1970s. However, that didn't last very long. Neighbors launched multiple complaints, including George Coombs, who told police that bullets from the rifle range were flying past his Buckout Road residence.

Today, the site houses the Harrison Department of Public Works and Waste Transfer. While it's off limits to the public, sometimes, when the trees are bare, you may catch a glimpse of the silos that once housed the lethal missiles.

Directly behind the Nike Missile site's remains, parallel to the remaining half-mile or so of Park Lane, is Woodman's Cove. The body of water is named after farmer Henry Woodman, who lived on Archer Hill in the village of Kensico. He went missing in 1891, and later that year, locals found his body in the murky waters of the cove that now bears his name. It remains unknown how Henry Woodman ended up in the water.

Woodman's Cove connects to the waters of adjacent Rye Lake, which now surround "Great Island," the former steep Archer's Hill of Kensico, NY. The water also connects with Kensico Reservoir, which flows over the lost village of Kensico, discussed at length in *Nightmarish Neighborhood #1.*

A few yards away from the former missile site, Park Lane intersects with Old Orchard Street near Cranberry Lake. In 1894, witnesses reported seeing a strange gorilla-like cryptid creature there. That spooky encounter and many other odd and tragic events are discussed at length in *Nightmarish Neighborhood #2.*

Old Orchard Street, which includes some remnants of the lost village of Kensico, runs down and, at times, parallel to Buckout Road, with nothing but thick woods between them. With such close proximity, all three nightmarish neighborhoods may share some spooky haunts

18.) THE LEATHERMAN

Caves litter the thick woods surrounding Old Orchard Street and Buckout Road, but one, in particular, has an eerie history dating back to the Revolutionary War. It's also rumored to be haunted by a spirit protecting a hidden stash of gold.

According to local lore, General George Washington's Continental Army used this particular cave to store ammunition during the Revolutionary War. After the war, one of the soldiers responsible for transporting the ammunition began living in the cave like a hermit after discovering his wife had left him for another man. Eventually, locals began referring to him as "Old Man Pops," leading to the cave being unofficially named Pop's Cave.

Beyond being tied to the Revolutionary War, Pop's Cave is also rumored to have played a role in the operations of the Underground Railroad. It's believed that fugitive slaves may have hidden in the area of Stony Hill, including Pop's Cave, before continuing north through nearby Connecticut and eventually Canada.

Odd abodes were typical in the neighborhood centuries ago. Nearby, Old Orchard Street hermit Jimmy-Under-The-Rock lived near the reservoir in a makeshift rock shelter . According to local oral tradition, there used to be an old dirt cellar on the right-hand side of Old Lake Street, off Buckout Road, where a very old Black man lived. It's said that when the Patriots rode through to warn the neighborhood of the

British coming, they backed their horses up to the door, kicked it in, and scared the old man nearly to death.

During the mid-1800s, it's believed that Pop's Cave became home to the famous wandering hobo, The Leatherman. Dressed in homemade leather pants up to his chest with suspenders, a long heavy leather coat, and wooden shoes, he came to the doors of farm kitchens between the 1850s and 1880s looking for handouts of food and tobacco.

His leather suit reportedly weighed around 60 pounds, and he wore it even on the hottest summer days. Little is known about the mysterious leather-clad man's identity, though some have speculated The Leatherman was Jules Bourglay of Lyons, France.

According to legend, Jules was the second son of a prominent French businessman. He grew up in a wealthy family and received a good education. As a young adult, he took charge of the family's extensive leather business and worked rigorously. After four successful and profitable years, the market for leather garments and gloves in Europe weakened dramatically, forcing Jules to lay off employees and go out of business.

Being driven out of business drove Jules insane. In the process, he also lost the opportunity to marry his true love, who viewed him as a failure. A heartbroken Jules packed a few belongings and his life savings of approximately $50,000 in gold coins (approx $1.5M modern) and headed for America. He was 25 years old.

After arriving in New York, Jules allegedly dressed in leather, purchased a single-wheeled wooden wheelbarrow. He loaded some supplies and several leather sacks that contained his gold coins. He spoke no English and only mumbled softly in French. He began to wander with no direction in mind, knocking on doors and asking for handouts.

If a leather-clad wandering hobo came knocking on doors in modern-day mumbling about free tobacco, he'd likely be arrested or shot. The Leatherman however, was treated like a celebrity. In fact, during the 1850s, families marked their calendars for his next visit, which occurred every 34 days.

"The Leatherman's Loop" stretched for over 300 miles and included towns in Westchester and Connecticut. Merchants used photographs of the intriguing leather-clad man to advertise goods in their shops, making him perhaps the first influencer or product endorser.

Sadly, on March 24, 1889, a local man named Henry Miller discovered The Leatherman dead inside a cave on George Dell's farm in Mt. Pleasant, NY, near a modern-day Girl Scout camp on Chappaqua Road in Briarcliff, NY. The shocking death, ruled to be caused by mouth cancer, made front-page news.

The Globe Museum in New York City purchased his leather outfit. The museum dressed a man in Leatherman's clothes who growled, "I am hungry. Give me a child to eat," which sparked protests.

The beloved Leatherman was buried in a simple pine box under a used tombstone in Ossining, NY. The identity of the wanderer, who walked with a cane and carried a leather bag with an ax and a French prayer book, remained unknown. In 1953, his headstone was changed to:

"Final resting place of Jules Bourglay of Lyons France. The Leatherman Who walked a 365-mile loop through Westchester and Connecticut from the Connecticut River to the Hudson, living in caves in 1858–1889."

In 2011, the Ossining Historical Society decided to move The Leatherman's remains. O.H.S. President Norman MacDonald said it was for safety concerns as the original grave was in the pauper's section of Sparta Cemetery next to a bustling area of Route 9. Their plan to take DNA became controversial as The Leatherman never let anyone know his true identity.

Connecticut historian Dan DeLuca was a driving force in searching for The Leatherman's remains. He believes that the famed wanderer has been falsely identified as Jules Bourglay and thus believes his gravesite should reflect the name on his death certificate, The Old Leatherman. Mr. DeLuca gave an interview in 2010 and stated that many people's ideas about The Leatherman needed to be more accurate. He said that The Leatherman would talk to people in French, never beg for food, and wasn't a tramp or hobo. He also mentioned that Leatherman knew Native American lore, knew how to preserve food, fish, and tan leather, and had several gardens at various locations.

Regardless of controversies, on May 24, 2011, Connecticut archaeologist Dr. Nicholas Bellantoni supervised an exhumation of The Leatherman's gravesite. Experts believed it contained the remains of the famous mysterious wanderer, which could lead to DNA testing. But that wasn't the case. The only thing remaining in the old pine box was a few old coffin nails, which they reburied a few days later in a new grave site located a few yards further from Route 9 in Ossining's Sparta Cemetery. The stone's new epitaph reads: "The Leatherman."

It remains unknown where The Leatherman hid his purported fortune of gold coins or if the treasure ever existed. Some claim he stashed them in his favorite cave. Could that be Pop's Cave on Buckout Road? Some have even claimed to see The Leatherman's ghost in the woods of Buckout Road, perhaps guarding his loot.

Tales of The Leatherman have captivated many, including Pearl Jam singer Eddie Vedder. During a 1998 Pearl Jam performance at Madison Square Garden, Eddie shared a story:

"So two Christmases ago, I was staying with a good friend somewhere on the outskirts outside the city, outside of the traffic, and this next song is written about this guy we learned about on this hike we took. We took this hike and out on these back trails, and this guy used to set up these little caves, ya know rock caves, and he had them all spread around for like ten miles. Just every night, go to a different cave. Each one just a few miles away from the other. So the next song is written about him. This is Leatherman."

In the 1930s, a Civilian Conservation Corp camp built large stone steps leading to Pop's Cave, known locally as the "Stairway to Heaven," perhaps as an homage to those who may have visited.

Perhaps drawing influence from infamous eccentric locals like The Leatherman, Old Man Pops, and Jimmy-Under-The-Rock, in the 1940s, a White Plains man named Charles Jones moved into an abandoned cellar on the site of a former shack on Stoney Brook Road. When Harrison Police ordered Mr. Jones and his wife to vacate the premises, he told them he had squatters rights and posed for a newspaper photograph with his pal Walter Coombs, who lived around the corner on Buckout Road.

 The town of Harrison eventually purchased part of the former Stony Hill community land to repurpose as a park. While shacks and makeshift dwellings decorated the Buckout Road area, just about a mile down Old Lake Street, behind Stony Hill Cemetery, was the hustle and bustle of Silver Lake Park next to Silver Lake in downtown West Harrison.

19.) SILVER LAKE

During the early years of the 20th century, the addition of hotels, a casino, and a famous ski jump transformed the downtown West Harrison area near Silver Lake into a tourist destination.

During the Revolutionary period, Silver Lake was known as Horton's Pond. The name derived from John Horton's family, who established a mill operated by water power from the pond, which was formed by damming the Mamaroneck River. During the Revolutionary War, George Washington's Continental Army used Horton's Mill to store supplies, triggering several enemy skirmishes.

For many years, the land at the southern end of Horton's Pond was known as Brown's Point, a small piece of land independent of surrounding White Plains and Harrison. Over time, however, the boundaries blurred, and the land became part of the neighboring areas.

Horton's Pond was passed down through the generations until it became renamed St. Mary's Lake sometime during the 1800s. In the 1890s, a visionary developer named Samuel Gainsbourg bought the property and renamed it Silver Lake. The area briefly became a summer resort, with a casino near the lake where the modern-day baseball field is located. The row of shops where Silver Lake Pizza and Fast Freddy's barbershop are currently located used to be the site of stables and a hotel.

Unfortunately, as the area began to transform in the late 19th century, numerous tragedies, including the following dozen events, started to occur.

I.)

In July 1885, a Tarrytown man named Harvey Robbins became intoxicated and interfered with William Horton's farm hands. When Robbins saw an arresting officer coming for him, he plunged into St. Mary's Lake, swam out, threw his hands up, and sank. A day later, searchers recovered his body.

II.)

A few years later, in August 1892, Jacob Breitmoser drowned in St. Mary's Lake while riding a horse. He worked as one of the supervisors on C. Deutermanns & Son's farm in present-day downtown West Harrison. It's believed when the horse began to sink, it threw Jacob off and kicked him, leaving him insensible.

III.)

Men working at the nearby park succeeded in saving a local servant named Lizzie O'Shea, who tried to drown herself in the lake in June 1893 purposely. After she was pulled ashore, the police jailed her for attempted suicide.

IV.)

In 1896, the grove around St. Mary's Lake added a merry-go-round and a fine dining restaurant. During the off-season, the lake became popular for ice skating. In February 1899, 23-year-old Charles F. James and 19-year-old P.H. Anderson fell through the ice while skating on St. Mary's Lake and drowned.

V.)

In 1905, 17-year-old Thomas Engler and 45-year-old George Huber drowned in St. Mary's Lake while having an outing with a number of their friends. When out on the lake, the friends tried to transfer from one boat to another, causing the boats to capsize and sink.

VI.)

A young painter named Gilbert Stephens, possibly a descendant of the Quaker Stephens family who resided on Buckout Road, made the local news multiple times, including once when he survived shooting himself. While staying at the house of William Francis, he allegedly attempted suicide after William's wife declined, wanting to run off with him.

A few years later, in 1910, Stephens, who lived in the Silver Lake Park section of town, had to be rescued after almost drowning in quicksand. One evening, he cut home along the north side of the lake, which is nearly dry and practically a mud hole, but, at the crossing, he began to sink, slowly almost buried up to his neck.

VII.)

In September 1910, panic spread through town as the lake owners drained it. According to the water company, the drainage was necessary to clean the lake's bed. The drainage caused the death of thousands of fish, including large carp weighing up to 20 pounds each.

VIII.)

Beyond ice skating at the lake in the 1920s, Harrison, NY residents were accustomed to staying indoors during the winter season; however, a group of Norwegians who moved into town dared to change that. In 1927, ski jumping, another winter sport, made its way to Silver Lake in Harrison, just down the street from Buckout Road.

For two months, locals watched the giant ski jump wood structure along Woodside Avenue take shape until it reached completion.

It soared 90 feet high with a slanted sliding chute. At 118 feet, the ski jump became one of the longest landing hills on the East Coast. When the United States Eastern Amateur Ski Association sanctioned the area, the Norway Ski Club prepared for its first competition in February 1928. Then catastrophe struck.

"Two weeks before the event, a fierce windstorm blew down the trestle, which the club members had not supported with guide wires. While the structure was somewhat intact, the main support timbers had splintered off and were now stuck out of the ground like giant toothpicks," recalled resident Mr. Barrego in an article from the White Plains Ski

Club's 1957 newsletter. He continued, *"Soon, the hill swarmed with men and echoed with the sound of hammers, saws, and the grunt of heavy labor. In two weeks, the trestle was back up, this time with strong guy wires holding it firmly in place."*

Jump Sunday arrived. "It was cold and extremely windy," Mr. Barrego wrote.

"Nevertheless, carloads of people from miles around made their way to Silver Lake. Admission was $1, but with no barriers or crowd control, 5,000 spectators surrounded the run-out area at the base of the hill, stamping their feet and thrashing their arms to keep warm."

Thirty jumpers competed, including redheaded Norwegian Chris Hoidalen, who jumped first after downing a shot of whisky from a flask.

The ski jump and local casino turned the Silver Lake area near Buckout Road into a tourist destination. New hotels emerged, including the Comerford Brothers Harrison Hotel near Silver Lake and the Holland House Hotel on Lake Street, where the trolley would start at White Plains. Local business boomed until 1949, when a hurricane destroyed the ski jump.

IX.)

In June 1931, near the border of Harrison and White Plains, an unknown assailant shot 35-year-old Silver Lake laborer Antonio Campanella. Antonio refused to tell the police who shot him, which raised suspicions, especially as the incident occurred shortly after the fatal mafia shootout at nearby Gretna Green Tavern, as discussed in *Nightmarish Neighborhood #2*. Antonio died from the two bullet wounds. The Medical Examiner ruled his death an unsolved murder.

X.)

In April 1961, several children under 15 were fishing on the west side of Silver Lake near the Dellwood Dairy Plant. It's unclear if they caught any fish that day, but they did make a gruesome discovery: a dead body. The police recovered the remains of 75-year-old Jose Oyarzun, who they said often went for walks around the lake.

XI.)

Local man Levi Best perpetually made local news headlines. Unfortunately, it was usually for horrible reasons like threatening a neighbor with a kitchen knife in front of his house, getting bitten by a stray dog, and stabbing a man during an argument.

 Other times, it was for bizarre reasons, like the time he told the police his brother had been killed in White Plains during the night and the time that he saw his wife run over by a truck. Neither of which was true.

Another time, he slipped and fell off a railroad platform as an engine and two cars passed. The train engineer, believing the train had hit the man, had an ambulance called. When they arrived, Levi was unharmed.

The fascinating individual, who the police also arrested numerous times for vagrancy and disorderly conduct, met his grim end in 1961, when detectives found his body, drowned in St. Mary's Lake. They said there was no evidence of foul play, though perhaps, as with any instance with Levi Best, anything is possible.

XII.)
 The town of Harrison opened a small zoo in 1965 down the street from Buckout Road near Silver Lake. The zoo featured a popular monkey named Cocoa, Calvin the giant snapping turtle, and various small animals enjoyed by the local community. Unfortunately, tragedy struck in 1971 when three youths, all sons of policemen, were arrested that August for killing and mutilating the animals.

 Zoo maintenance man John Mederios stated,
 "I opened the place and saw this big slaughter out there. Everything was splattered all over the place."

Animals had been skinned, plucked, or dismembered. A pair of rabbit ears hung over the doorknob of the entrance to the zoo's office.

Animal carcasses lay in front of the door and on the roof. Mutilated carcasses of 11 rabbits, three pigeons, and a chicken were discarded around the zoo. The only survivors were a guinea pig, a rooster, and Cocoa, the monkey discovered in a nearby tree with bruises.

20.) THE REAL HEADLESS HORSEMAN

Perched between serene Silver Lake and historic Buckout Road, Merritt Hill is a testament to the Revolutionary War, a pivotal era that shaped our history. This site, named after its owner during the early 1700s, Daniel Merritt, is not just a hill but a living chronicle of our past.

The Merritts were a prominent Westchester family with descendants who played roles on both sides of the Revolutionary War, including the feared murderous outlaw discussed at length in *Nightmarish Neighborhood #2,* Shubael Merritt, who rode through Westchester County with various notorious marauding gangs, including Emmerich's Chasseurs and the dreaded DeLancey's Cowboys, plundering all those in their path throughout what was declared "The Neutral Ground" between the bases of the British and American armies.

George Washington's Continental Army and General William Howe's British forces, combined with units of hired German mercenaries called Hessians, fought on October 28, 1776, in what became known as The Battle of White Plains.

While the Patriots and Redcoats had clashed previously, this was the first time the Continental Army had to fight the Hessians, who were greatly feared during the Revolution.

These German soldiers were sent to America to reinforce the British Army. Hessians got their name as many of these men were from Hesse-Kassel in Germany. The foreign-speaking warriors were viewed as bloodthirsty killers and easily vilified in America. They were renowned as fearsome fighters, and there were stories that they showed no quarter to retreating American troops, including rumors of nailing Patriot riflemen to trees with their bayonets.

When Washington's troops arrived in White Plains in late October 1776, they strategically positioned themselves on various hilltops, including Miller Hill and Travis Hill off North Broadway in North White Plains, Mount Misery near Old Orchard Street, Hatfield Hill on Hall Avenue / Buckout Road, and Merritt Hill adjacent to Buckout Road. The elevated vantage point allowed them to track enemy movements and launch attacks from higher ground.

General Washington headquartered at a home in North White Plains. General William Heath, who commanded the left flank of the Continental Army, headquartered at the Hatfield House on Buckout Road, with his troops encamped nearby.

Leading up to the Battle of White Plains, the Continental Army stretched out for nearly three miles, covering the ground from downtown White Plains near Chatterton Hill to Silver Lake.

As discussed at length in *Nightmarish Neighborhood #2*, the main action of the Battle of White Plains took place on Chatterton Hill. During the fight, an estimated 500 men combined from both sides died in battle.

Both armies remained in the area after the battle, which led to multiple inevitable conflicts, including Gilbert Hatfield taking out multiple Hessian soldiers in a fistfight and Captain Tilton falling to his death at Mucklestone Rock while trying to capture General Heath.

At some point, the British Army discovered that Washington stored supplies at Horton's Mill on modern-day Lake Street across the street from Delfino Park. They, however, didn't realize that General Heath had stationed troops on Merritt Hill to defend it, including Lieutenant Ephraim Fenno, who was armed with a cannon.

There's a marker on Merritt Hill with the following caption:

Lt. Fenno fired a cannon ball directly into 20 British horsemen approaching Hatfield Hill. The single shot caused the British to retreat back towards White Plains.

The marker is located in the current Silver Lake Preserve parking lot around the corner from Buckout Road on Old Lake Street. The Silver Lake Preserve, like the adjacent Cranberry Lake Preserve, offers multiple hiking trails, many leading towards Stony Hill Cemetery and other points off Buckout Road.

While staying at the Hatfield House on Buckout Road, General Heath wrote in his journal about another incident on Merritt Hill that played out on October 31, 1776.

"Here, unknown to them were some 12 pounders, upon the discharge of which they made off with their field pieces as fast as their horses could draw them. A shot from the American cannon at this place took off the head of a Hessian artilleryman. They also left one of the artillery horses dead on the field. What other loss they sustained was not known."

Comrades of the fallen Hessian soldier referenced by General Heath took his body to be buried at the Old Dutch Burial Ground in North Tarrytown, NY, later renamed Sleepy Hollow. It remains unknown what happened to his decapitated head.

It's rumored that years later, a young man whose parents named him after General George Washington read about this intriguing incident at a library in nearby Tarrytown.

In addition to being named after George Washington, who he met when he was six years old, author Washington Irving had multiple attachments to the Revolution, which perhaps piqued his interest in reading about it as much as possible.

Born in early April 1783 in New York City, during the same week that marked the official British ceasefire, which concluded the war, Irving eventually lived in Tarrytown. His time in Westchester County perhaps inspired a legendary story.

Perhaps his most famous piece of writing, the 1819 short story "The Legend of Sleepy Hollow," introduced the world to America's earliest and most famous ghostly phantom, The Headless Horseman. Perhaps even spookier than the page's ghost stories that frightened the story's hero, Ichabod Crane, is the rumor that Irving based locations and characters in the classic tale on real life.

In the story, Irving refers to his iconic villain as

"the ghost of a Hessian trooper, whose head had been carried away by a cannonball, in some nameless battle during the Revolutionary War."

Irving continues,

"Having been buried in the churchyard, the ghost rides forth to the scene of battle in nightly quest for his head."

While Irving's fictional "Legend of Sleepy Hollow" revolves around The Headless Horseman tormenting local school teacher Ichabod Crane in Sleepy Hollow, the actual battle where the real-life basis for the Headless Horseman occurred, was on Merritt Hill, adjacent to Buckout Road.

For many years, Merritt Hill has been the site of an annual reenactment of The Battle of White Plains, featuring actors in authentic period clothing and weaponry. The remains of Horton's Mill, where General Washington stored supplies, still stand on Lake Street, though the building is now a private residence.

While the Horseman's head may still be missing, the cannonball that blew it off may be hiding in plain sight. According to local lore, when Gilbert Hatfield's patriotic cousin Daniel Hatfield renovated his home at the corner of Kensico Ave and Lake Street in 1786, they lined the house's double chimneys with locally recovered Revolutionary War cannonballs. The house with two chimneys has since been repurposed as a delicatessen. Outside La Puebla Deli, a marker reads, "Heritage Trail: Home of the Hatfields, Officers and Patriots under George Washington."

While it's unknown what quantities of fact or imagination went into creating The Headless Horseman on the pages of "The Legend of Sleepy Hollow" if the Horseman does emerge nightly from his grave at the Old Dutch Burial Ground and rides to the scene of the battle in search of his missing head, that means America's earliest and most famous ghostly phantom is patrolling the neighborhood of Buckout Road, an area rich in history and ghostly urban legends, before riding ten miles back to his gravesite in Sleepy Hollow.

Additional books from the *Nightmarish Neighborhood* series are available now on Amazon and BarnesAndNoble.com.

For more info, please visit:
BuckoutRoad.com and RightOnDudes.com